The Complete Guide to
Double-deck Pinochle

The definitive guidebook to playing
Double-deck Pinochle

by

L. RoyRam

Editorial review and formatting by D. J. Switzer

P/P

Copyright © 2004
PINOCHLE PRESS
P.O. BOX 120040
ST. ALBANS, NY 11412

Although the author, editor and publisher have made every effort to ensure the accuracy and completeness of information contained in this book, we assume no responsibility for errors, inaccuracies, omissions, or any inconsistencies herein. Any slights of people, places, or organizations are purely unintentional, or the result of an overactive imagination.

Printed and bound in the United States of America.

Library of Congress Cataloging-in-Publication Data
Ram, L. Roy ,
    The Complete Guide to Double Deck Pinochle /
L. Roy Ram

    Includes glossary and index ,

    Library of Congress Control Number: 2004109383
    ISBN 0-9742-090-0-7   (*Softcover Edition*)

<u>Foreword by Anthony Collins</u>
Author of 'Winning Pinochle Strategies'

After reviewing L. Roy Ram's "Complete Guide to Double-deck Pinochle", my reaction can be summed up in one word, "*Awesome*."

I admit to being somewhat skeptical when he asked me to give my opinion on his book. I figured I would give it the once over and send it back.

Once I opened the book however, I could tell right away he was a strong player, and his SCAMP bidding system.... well, it blew me away! I tried to punch holes in it, but the system is positive and irrefutably sound.

I was thinking, if I could get my group to adopt this system we would definitely have the upper hand on our competition.

I know the game, and believe me with his book and seminars, Ram has a lot to teach all of us.

INTRODUCTION

Although the seeds for this book were planted many years ago, I owe the green thumb for its germination to my brother, James, who encouraged me to use my surgery recuperation time to work on it, whence it took root. It is dedicated to my loving wife Lillie, who has given 43 of her best years to develop our family.

This book will serve as a learning legacy for all my children and grandchildren who learned to play Pinochle. Now they have a book to teach their children from.

I also acknowledge an unseen enemy who played a large part in the development of this book. Much of my time in the early years was spent playing Tournament Bridge where I was exposed to the second hand smoke, which caused my cancer. Without this catalyst I may have never been forced to write this book. May all my friends respect the air we all must breathe.

I would love to share your thoughts and experiences. To help me do so, see our Web site *www.PinochlePress.com* or send E-mail to *LRoyRam@PinochlePress.com*. Send your favorite story you would like to see included in the next book.

Attention: Corporations, Universities, Colleges, Clubs and professional organizations:

Quantity discounts are available on bulk purchases of this book for educational purposes or as premiums to renew magazine subscriptions or increase circulation. Special editions or book excerpts can also be created to fit your specific needs. For information please contact:

**PINOCHLE PRESS, P.O.BOX 120040
ST. ALBANS, NY 11412**

ACKNOWLEDGMENTS

Kudos for technical advice to *Leah*, *Tim*, *Dot* and *David Bailey*. Encouragement and partnership came from *Lydia James*.

Marriott 'Beau' Miller, *Henry Nelson*, *Eddie Lewis* and *Mario Foston* assisted with editorial advice.

For original cartoons we have *Kevin Owens*, *Juanita McLeod, Harry Duren* and *Douglas Switzer* to thank.

Photography shoots and stills are credited to *Carl 'The Colonel' Spooner* and *Ted Gerran*.

Publicity and Marketing by *The Rambo Group*

Douglas Switzer designed the cover.

Pinochle Press Advisory Board

TABLE OF CONTENTS

CARTOONS

PART 1 - IN THE BEGINNING
"We all have to start someplace."

"Where have you been boy, over at your Uncle Willie's playing cards again? I wish he'd teach you something practical."

My folks were not into cards. In my hometown of Washington, DC, the war effort had full influence in the early 1940's. People were working overtime in the defense industry, and leisure time was at a premium. My Uncle Willie worked for the federal government but had no hang-ups about recreation. He was both an accomplished jazz musician and man about town. Famous musicians were always coming by to 'jam' at his spacious home in the Northeast section. He was well known for his skills at checkers and chess, and he played Pinochle every day on his lunch breaks. It was his sideline hobby.

Pinochle was not new to the USA even then. Pinochle evidently is a variation of the French card game Bezique. Some historians have traced the game to a French card game called Piquet, first played in the 15th century. Others claim that a Swede invented it under another name during the early 1800's. In any case, Bezique finally turned up in Germany under the name Binochle, or Penuchle. It was later imported to the United States by German and Irish immigrants who settled in the Midwest during the latter half of the 19th century.

Its spread throughout the country is credited to the Armed Forces where it continues to be a staple form of recreation. These members picked up the game and returned it to their hometowns. Pinochle ranks after Bridge, as the second most popular four-handed card game in the United States.

My cousin and I wanted to try our skills and Uncle Willie was a willing instructor (whom we could never beat). So exposure to the game for close to 60 years, coupled with extensive travel in 40 States and 20 foreign countries, gives me some perspectives that I enjoy sharing with my students.

Whys and Wherefores

I guess what I like most about playing Pinochle all over the world is the sense that Pinochle is to me a fun, competitive game, rather than a gambling game. At the same time it offers an intellectual challenge equal to that of few other games. You can't help getting your blood up when an opponent sits down at the table, looks in your face, and places a brand-new tub of Whipping BUTTer in front of you. Especially when you know that the game offers more of a premium for skills than luck. I'm sure that a certain amount of luck or good fortune helps, but over time, what we call luck sort of evens itself out through the law of averages. So although we all look for fantastic hands, what more could you ask but to get the best out of whatever cards you were dealt? If that's your aim, then you've gotten 'lucky'; read on.

That's one purpose of this book. Another is to give the beginning player a starting point to learn this fascinating and captivating game. Along the way we will provide a repository of knowledge about the game and give a ready reference for terms and plays.

The third purpose chronicles my fight with cancer, caused by allowing myself to be exposed to secondhand cigarette smoke while playing cards. This was in the days when you had no recourse if you wanted to play serious cards on a national level. Of course there were tables even then at tournaments where smoking was banned, but smoke still filled the rooms. Anyone could tell where you had been, because your clothes were permeated with the reek of smoke. At the time we viewed it as a necessary evil, because we wanted to allow smokers their rights. Little did we know that our rights, as well as our bodies, were being violated in the process.

While in the hospital, I first developed my syndicated column, Pinochle Passion, which now appears in newspapers throughout the US and has done much to publicize the game. Many had no knowledge of the game before reading the column.

Of special value to many will be my **SCAMP** Bidding System, which has already modernized and updated Pinochle bidding on the Internet. This highly innovative system constitutes a major revision in the history of the game.

When Walter Gibson's book on Pinochle was written in 1974, it did not even include Double-deck Pinochle. Since then, Anthony Collins' book, *Winning Pinochle Strategies*, has increased awareness of the game. But I predict that Double-deck Pinochle will eventually become a world-class card game, like Bridge, as the duplicate aspect of the game comes into vogue.

This will open the way for competition at the college level, as well as simultaneous tournaments all around the world. We offer congratulations to you for joining us on the cutting edge of research into this exciting topic.

"Getting an Early Start"

Did you ever have a problem, as did I, when you were a little tyke, trying to get the "big boys" to let you play?

Maybe they were just a little bit worried that they might end up getting whupped, and they just couldn't take the chance.

The Pinochle Deck

Initially, we will give a brief overview of the game. Later in the book we will feature complete hands that may demonstrate differing styles of bidding, partnership defense, distributional concepts, play of the hand, or other advanced themes. To benefit fully from the information presented, readers should lay out the hands and follow the line of play suggested.

Pinochle is one of many trump games such as Spades, Whist, Euchre and Bridge. In Pinochle, we first lay out certain combinations of cards having point values. These are called melds. Afterwards we attempt to win tricks containing counter cards during play of the hand. Pinochle differs from most trump games mainly in the deck used. These are the cards in a regular Pinochle deck:

A A 10 10 K K Q Q J J 9 9

This is duplicated in four suits for a total of 48 cards. Note that the order of the cards is somewhat different from a regular deck, the 10 ranking below the ace, but above the other cards. If two cards of the same rank are played, the one played first has precedence.

To play Double-deck Pinochle you use two decks, but eliminate the 9's. 20 cards in each suit adds up to 80 cards.

A A A A 10 10 10 10 K K K K Q Q Q Q J J J J

Ram's Double-deck Cards are pre-packaged as a set of 80 cards in a single box, available at *www.PinochlePress.com*.

Basic Play

On each deal, you first Bid and Show the Meld, then you Play the Hand. First, we will briefly discuss the rules of bidding, what cards constitute the meld, and general rules of playing the hands. This will be amplified later in the book.

Bidding

Bidding starts with the player to the dealers left, and it proceeds in auction style until three of the players have passed. Bids must name a number 50 or higher. The lowest bid possible is 50. There is no upper limit to how high you may bid. Bids between 50 and 60 may be made at any point along the scale, but once the bidding reaches 60, all bids must be made in increments of at least 5 points. For example, you may bid 60, 65, or 70, but not 63, 68 or 71. If you do not wish to bid for any reason, you must say *"Pass"* or *"No Bid."* Once you pass, you may not re-enter the bidding on that particular hand.

To be valid, a bid must be higher than any previous bid. The bidding or auction comes to an end when all three of the other players have passed. Auction means that you may have more than one chance to bid. The bidding may go around the table many times as long as another player chooses to make a higher bid. The person making the final bid has the right to name the trump suit. The player bidding highest must show at least a marriage (king and queen) in the suit named as trump, along with the rest of the meld. All other players then lay down their meld cards. Cards used in meld combinations carry specific point values.

What is Meld?

Here are examples of meld you may hold[1]:

Card combination	Point Value
King & Queen in each suit	24
Run of A~10~K~Q~J in the trump suit	15
Ace in each suit	10
King in each suit	8
Queen in each suit	6
Jack in each suit	4

Meld cards must be exposed on the table for inspection. Partners need a minimum of 20 Meld between them for their side to receive meld credit. After Meld is shown and recorded, all players pick up their cards and Play of the Hand starts.

Play of the Hand

The Declarer, or high bidder plays first as the players in turn clockwise, follow suit on the trick, or book. The player with the highest card takes the book and leads to the next trick. After all 20 tricks have been played; both sides total all Aces, Tens and Kings contained in their combined tricks. These are High Card Points (HCP) and total up to 48. Also, the side winning the last trick receives a 2 point bonus. Thus, the highest possible total HCP is 50 points.

If the bidding team fail to make a 20 HCP minimum, they forfeit their meld for that hand, and the amount of the bid is deducted from their score as a penalty. Defenders who fail to make 20 HCP forfeit any meld recorded for that hand. The first team to reach 500, or another pre-set amount, wins the game. However, note a variation under *Bidding Out to Win the Game* on page 215.

---

[1] A more complete Meld Chart is available later in this chapter and in the Appendix.

Follow Suit or Head Up?

Another major difference in this trump game is the rule that on every trick led, each player if possible must *"Head up,"* or *"Cover,"* the trick (play a higher card than the ones already on the trick). This presents a challenge to players accustomed to games such as Bridge, Whist or Spades. In those games players have the option of playing high or low as they see fit.

For example, in most other games, if your partner or another player has already played a high card on a trick you may elect to play high or low on the trick. Not so in Pinochle. To help understand this concept, the rules for play of the hand are outlined below:

1. If you have any card in the suit that was led, you must *"Follow Suit,"* playing a card of that suit.

2. If you hold any card in your hand higher than those on the trick at the time it reaches you, you must *"Head Up,"* or *"Cover,"* the trick, thus play a higher card. If you do not have the suit led, but you have a trump card, you must play a trump. If there is a trump already played on the trick, you must play a higher one if you can.[2]

3. If you have no cards in the suit led and you have a trump card of any value, even if it is not high enough to take the trick, when it is your turn to play you must still play a trump card.

4. If you do not have the suit led and you do not have any trump cards, you may *"Throw Off,"* or *"Discard,"* any card, in any other suit.

---

[2]In some localities you must "cover" on trump leads, but not off-suit. Also, some do not require you to overtrump when trump has not been led. Variations exist, so check for local customs before play begins.

In Pinochle we are not permitted to *"Hold Up"* if a lower card is led. For example, suppose we hold A~10~J~J~J, and our opponent holds A~A~A~10~10 in the same suit. If the opponent played the three aces, we would play our jacks on the three aces, thus making sure of two winning tricks for us. However, if the opponent led a ten first, we have no choice but to play our ace, and we are thus restricted to getting only a single trick.

In Pinochle, no suit outranks another, except for the trump suit named in each hand. However, in this book, we usually place the spade and heart suits first in our diagrams, then the club suit along with the diamond suit below them. This alternation of red and black colored suits is simply to present a consistent view of the hands.

You will note that in Pinochle all hands are played with a trump suit, as there is no concept of playing in no-trump. During play of the hand, any card in the trump suit always outranks all cards in any other suit. If players have no cards in the suit led, then they must play a trump if they have one, if not they may discard a card from another suit. If the trick is won or about to be won by your partner, you may want to play a counter card on it (king, ten or ace) whereas if the trick is going to your opponents, you may discard a non-counter (queen or jack).

For example, with spades as trump, if a heart is played and you have no hearts in your hand, you must play a spade if you have any. Any spade, whether high or low, ranks higher than the hearts and will win the trick. Again, if someone has already trumped a trick that you must trump, you must play a higher trump than the one already played if you can. This is true even if your partner has played the other trump. You must go higher if possible. Also remember, if unable to play higher, you must still play a trump if you have any remaining.

Many new Double-deck Pinochle players ask: *"We get 20 cards? Why so many?"* Originally the double-deck was trimmed down from 96 to 80 cards. Imagine holding 24 cards! Truly, Double-deck Pinochle is a step up, in the amount of cards and in complexity of the game, over Single-deck Pinochle.

Many Pinochle enthusiasts cut their teeth on trump games like Spades and Whist. Most previous Whist players avoid Whist once they learn Pinochle. Certainly Spades players who convert to Whist seldom go back. The only trump game more complex is Bridge. However, Pinochle enjoys a greater percentage of new players nation wide, because it is much easier to learn than Bridge.

Reading Between the Lines

As you go through the book, you will notice many places where there are curly braces around one or more exclamation marks {!} or question marks {?}, and you might wonder, *"What's this?"* You will notice these most often when play of the hands is described. Here is a short explanation to keep in mind when you see these little reminders.

- {!} means this was a good play or bid.
- {!!} indicates that this was an outstanding play.
- {?} would show this was a questionable play. (Your partner might ask, *"Why did you do that?"*)
- {??} simply means this was an absolutely horrendous play. (Your partner may just ask, *"Whose partner are you anyway?"*)

Do you often get {?} and {??}, but seldom {!} and {!!}?

"Playing a Short Game"
"We get to change
partners after this.
Right?"

Did you ever have one of those partners you just couldn't get rid of? And people would rather go home than get stuck with him? The only time I really feel bad is when playing cutthroat and the partner I want to get rid of is myself. Then, no matter how short the game is, it's just too long.

CHAPTER 1 - GETTING STARTED
"Don't Forget to Have Fun"

Having become familiar with the deck, let's set up to play. We certainly don't want to insult anyone's intelligence, so feel free to skip over this section, as it is written for those brand new at the game (*This part is not rocket science.*)

We'll ask you now to open up four single Pinochle decks, two red and two blue, making sure to remove all the nines as well as any extraneous advertising cards. You will not be needing these extra cards so throw them away, but keep the boxes for storage after the game. Of course you could avoid this extra trouble by using Ram's prepackaged double-decks available on our Web site *www.PinochlePress.com*.

Shuffle two decks of the same color together, and spread them face down on the table. (*You can skip this part if you have already decided on partners.*) Each of the players may choose for partners by picking a card from the deck. Players drawing the two highest cards (remember that the ten is next to the ace) are partners and get to select their seats and the color deck they will deal for the game, while players picking low cards get whatever's left. If three players pick equal cards, those three try again for high card until there are two high and two low. (*See, it's not so hard.*)

After partners are chosen, the dealer shuffles two decks of the same color together and allows his Right Hand Opponent (RHO) to cut. The Dealer starts at his left and deals the cards to each player in sets of four or five, (no more, no less) until everyone has 20 cards. Meanwhile the Left Hand Opponent (LHO) should shuffle the other two decks in preparation for his deal of the next hand. After dealing the first hand, the original dealer will cut the cards for the second hand.

Sorting the Cards

More Rocket Science. I admit that handling 20 cards is much harder than 5, 12 or 13 if you are used to Euchre, Spades, Whist or Bridge. Having observed others sort cards over the years, I will recommend one method that stands out as superior to me. Any other method may be superior to you. I'm sure it's in the eye of the beholder. I find that picking up the cards as they are dealt works best for me. This way I keep up with the count as I receive them and never pick up more than 20, even if the dealer makes a mistake. We emphasize, *Count Your Cards* before you have looked at all 20.

Nothing can be more disconcerting than having a double run firmly fixed in your mitt, then discovering that you hold one too many cards. Unfortunately since you already looked at your cards, they must be redealt. No Problem, hunh? Yeah, Right! Over my dead body, OK?

Anyway, as I pick up the cards with one hand I count each one. As I count them, I place them in the other hand in two places. All red cards go in the front, black cards in the back.

Now all 20 cards are in one hand, already sorted into two groups, red and black. I do this one more time, transferring the cards into the other hand by suits. I place hearts in the front and diamonds in the rear. Getting down to the black cards, I place spades in the front and clubs in the rear.

All 20 cards are now sorted into suits so I only have to arrange each suit. Here's where I try to get creative by always alternating the order and placement of each suit. One time I'll put the spades first, then hearts, clubs and diamonds. Another time we place the hearts first, then clubs, diamonds and spades.

Sometimes I'll line my cards up: A~10~K~K~Q~Q~J. At other times I'll place them in my hand in reverse order, thus: J~Q~Q~K~K~10~A.

This is just in case some sidewinder is watching where I'm pulling my cards from. He can't always tell what I have left by watching my hands. By the way, it's unethical to watch someone's hand in this manner. But like they tell the boxers: *"Break when I say break! But Protect Yourself at All Times."*

Protect yourself at the table by holding your cards up and away from the table. Any time your cards are spread and your hand is resting on the table, you are inviting someone to look at your cards. Some who are too lazy to hold up their cards have retorted: *"They may see them, but they can't play them."* How shortsighted! Even if they can't play <u>yours</u>, they certainly can play <u>theirs</u> better if you let them see yours. And why would you want to help the opponents? They're already getting help from your partner, OK? Anyway, you know what they told you in the first grade? *"I'll let you see mine if you let me see yours."* *"But you first!"* You remember what happened after that. Once they see yours, you never do get to see theirs.

Once your hand is sorted and protected, count your meld. Start with your shortest suit. If you have no ace, king, queen, or jack in that suit, then your only meld can be marriages, pinochles, or a run. If however, you do have an ace, king, queen or jack in the short suit, see if it is duplicated in the other three suits. If so, it is part of your meld.

On the next page there is a handy chart showing the point values for melds. The chart is duplicated in other places, with a more detailed one located in the appendix. The next chapter will give a fuller explanation of meld.

Introducing Meld

	SINGLE	DOUBLE	TRIPLE
PINOCHLE[3]	4[4, 6]	30	45 / 90[4]
JACKS	4	40	80
QUEENS	6	60	120
KINGS	8	80	160
ACES	10	100	200
RUN[5]	15[6]	150	300
ROUNDHOUSE[7]	24	240	
MARRIAGE	2	4	6
ROYAL MARRIAGE	4	8	12

I like to start counting my meld with the roundhouse if I have one. Next I count my aces, kings, queens and jacks, finally my pinochles. Hey! Maybe that's why I miss double pinochle sometimes. Maybe I lose count before I get to the pinochles.

I don't mind admitting that even an expert sometimes misses meld. It isn't because I don't know better, it's just that some mornings I forget to take my ASP's. We suggest that you buy, and keep, a ready supply of these on hand if you expect to be good at this game. As I mentioned earlier, this is a game of skill. Your skill will be enhanced considerably with a regular dose of Anti-Stupid Pills.

---

[3]Pinochle is the combination of a Jack of Diamonds and a Queen of Spades. Both cards must be in the same player's hand to count as a Pinochle.
[4]As agreed upon in advance of play or by local acceptance.
[5]The combination of a Run in trump and a Roundhouse is usually accepted as 35 points, not the anticipated 39 points.
[6]In the Florida System, played in the National Pinochle Association (NPA), a Run counts as 25 points and a Pinochle counts as 15 points.
[7]A Roundhouse is the combination of a King and Queen in each suit.

You might want to copy or clip out the meld chart in the Appendix. Laminate it and use for a ready reference as you read since it is more comprehensive. There is also one that you can laminate as a bookmark.

Counting Meld as Opener or as Responder

As you count your meld, consider whether you will be a an Opener/Declarer or a Responder. Declarers usually want to take the final bid so they can name trump because they have a long suit or a two-suited hand. A Responder normally has an even hand with no long suit to be made trump. Or maybe the long suit has no marriage in it and can't be named as trump.

Take a look at the following sample hands:

Sample Hand 1a:

Here you want to be Declarer because you have a two-suited hand and two aces in danger of being caught. Bid 50 if you are in first seat. If the opponents open the bidding, simply overcall (bid one over) the last bid.

Sample Hand 1b:

Again you want control of the hand because of your strong spades (nine card trump suit). First you send a meld bid to show your strength. We recommend you bid 2 over the last bid to show 20 meld. On your next turn you will bid again based on your partner's response.

Sample Hand 1c:

This is a weak hand to open as Declarer. Your hand is flat, that is, too evenly distributed. Your trump suit is not strong or long enough. You should either be a defender or support your partner if your partner has a biddable suit. That makes you a Responder; therefore, send your meld of 20 by bidding <u>two over</u> whatever the last bid was. (We'll discuss sending meld later.)

Sample Hand 1d:

Would you prefer to name a trump, or would you rather defend against someone else who made hearts or clubs trump? Yes, you have a defensive hand or a supportive hand if your partner can take the bid. Let partner know your strength by sending a meld bid of 30.

To summarize, if you have a long strong trump or have a two-suited hand, your hand may be suited for taking the bid. When your hand is even, consider a support role or defense.

Lessons Learned - A Declarer Hand or A Responder Hand?	
Declarer	**Responder**
➢ Long, Strong, Biddable Suit (eight or more trump, preferably with run) ➢ Two Suited Hand (3 - 6 cards in off suits)	➢ Even Hands (4, 5 or 6 cards in all suits) ➢ Power Hands (Aces) ➢ Strong Suits without Marriages

"Elementary Mathematics"

Unlike some other games, each side of the team can only count the cards in that person's hand toward meld. Then the partners get to total up what each one has individually.

CHAPTER 2 - COUNTING MELD WITH SCAMP
"Rx: Pinochle P.R.N. OTC. No known harmful side effects"

In the first chapter we mentioned two phases of the game, relevant to each hand; Bidding with Show of Meld, and Play of the Hand. Let's provide a little overview of these two phases before we get into counting meld.

Bidding and Show of Meld

There is a correlation between Bidding and Show of Meld. You must first become familiar with Meld values before you can begin bidding. Knowing the value of your hand gives you the ammunition to bid with.

The partnership that bids highest gets to name the trump suit. Having your long suit as trumps should give your side an advantage. It is in your interest then, to communicate with your partner, giving each other as much information as possible about the value, strength and shape of your hands. This will help your team to decide how high to bid.

On each new hand you are dealt, examine it looking for card combinations called meld. Based on the value of this meld coupled with power in your hand (aces), you determine whether your hand is suited for taking the bid (offense), defending against opponents, or supporting your partners' bid.

After the bid is won, both partnerships, before play of the hand starts, display their meld face-up on the table. Teams receive conditional credit for this *meld,* provided that the partnership collects at least 20 High Card Points (HCP) during play of the hand. High Card Points are earned by counting all *Aces*, *Tens* and *Kings* on books that each team wins during play.

The melds are then applied to the partnership score along with the HCP that they collected during the play of that hand.

Partners must show a combined meld of at least 20, for meld to be counted in that hand. Partners who show no meld still receive credit for HCP when they collect at least 20 HCP.

If no attempt is made to play a hand, no HCP can be collected by either team. Sometimes a bidder may decide to *"throw in the hand"* and go set, to prevent the opposition from scoring their meld. This subject is discussed later in the book.

Counting High Card Points (HCP) After Play

After melding and play of the hand, partnerships receive credit for their melds based on their collecting at least 20 of the HCP as shown below. Partners who show no meld still receive credit for HCP whenever they collect at least 20 HCP.

```
16 Aces:....1 point each...16 total points
16 Tens:.. .1 point each...16 total points
16 Kings:...1 point each...16 total points
Last Trick:.2 points        2 total points
Total Possible Points......50 total points
```

One fascinating twist to the game should be mentioned here. It is extremely rare for one partnership to collect all 50 HCP (every ace, ten and king, and also the last trick).

We call this a *"Trickless,"* and count it as a game win, regardless of the previous score. Make sure this is agreed upon before the game, as some do not consider this a win, for example Yahoo!, on the Internet. Note that it's still a "Trickless" even if the other team actually does get one of the first 19 tricks without a point on it.

Which Cards Make up Meld?

Plain Marriage: K and Q of any suit...........................2 pts
Royal Marriage; K and Q of trumps..........................4 pts

Run or Sequence in Trump suit: A~10~K~Q~J.............**15 pts**

Pinochle:	Q♠ and J◊............................4 pts	
Double Pinochle:	Q♠ Q ♠ and J◊ J◊......................30 pts	
Triple Pinochle:	Q♠ Q♠ Q♠ and J◊ J◊ J◊......**45 or 90 pts**	
Quadruple Pinochle:	Wins the game	

(If holder's team gets 20 HCP during hand play.)

Aces: One in each suit.......................................10 pts
　　　　Two in each suit.......................................100 pts
　　　　Three in each suit...................................**200 pts**

Kings: One in each suit.......................................8 pts
　　　　Two in each suit.......................................80 pts
　　　　Three in each suit...................................160 pts

Queens: One in each suit.......................................6 pts
　　　　Two in each suit.......................................60 pts
　　　　Three in each suit...................................120 pts

Jacks: One in each suit ....4 pts
　　　　Two in each suit.......................................40 pts
　　　　Three in each suit...................................80 pts

Roundhouse: A marriage in each suit.......................24 pts
　　　　　　Two marriages in each suit................240 pts

Run (in Trump) and Roundhouse:.......................**35 pts**

Meld Point Variations

Variations exist, in local and house rules about meld, so don't forget to agree upon the specific values before beginning a game. We showed the most frequent variations on the previous page in bold print. One such variation requires players to declare possession of aces around, regardless of whether they have 20 to meld. This is done by simply informing the table aloud: "*I have aces,*" anytime before the start of hand play. (See ACES, in the Glossary.)

Many meld tables show the values for quadruple (four of each) aces, kings, queens and jacks around. We generally won't bother to show those combinations in our meld tables[8] since the odds against it happening are quite preposterous.

MELD Summary Chart

	SINGLE	DOUBLE	TRIPLE
PINOCHLE	4[9]	30	45 / 90[9]
JACKS	4	40	80
QUEENS	6	60	120
KINGS	8	80	160
ACES	10	100	200
RUN[10]	15[11]	150	300
ROUNDHOUSE[12]	24	240	
MARRIAGE	2	4	6
ROYAL MARRIAGE	4	8	12

---

[8]We show values for these combinations in the more comprehensive meld table in the Appendix, for reference purposes.
[9]As agreed upon in advance of play or local acceptance.
[10]The combination of a Run in trump and a Roundhouse is usually accepted as 35 points, not the anticipated 39 points.
[11]In the Florida System, played in the National Pinochle Association, NPA, a Run counts as 25 points and a Pinochle counts as 15 points.
[12]A Roundhouse is the combination of a King and Queen in each suit.

RAM's SCAMP Bidding System

You have now arrived at the most controversial point in the entire book. A leopard must have good reasons to rub away it's spots as it can be rather painful. If you are a dyed in the wool Pinochle player from the old school, you may find the *SCAMP* Bidding System to be a bit radical. We only suggest that you approach it with an open mind and evaluate it objectively, comparing its merits against the old standard.

How does the system work? My system of Pinochle bidding uses the acronym *SCAMP*, to identify five factors by which to evaluate a hand.

S or *Shape* of the hand includes extra points for long trumps and long suits

C is for the minimum 20 *Count*, of high cards from trick play

A, is for *Aces*, which give power and control of the hand

M is for *Meld*, of which we never get enough.

P is for *Partner*, whose meld we always expect

SHAPE

Shape is the length of trump[13] and side suits. A bidder who has at least seven trump cards, may count 3 points for each trump more than the seven and count 3 points for each card more than five in a side suit. Consider the following hand:

A 10 10 K Q Q J J ♠ K Q ♡ A 10 K Q J ♣ A K Q J J ◇

In this hand, you count only 3 points for *Shape* as you do have an 8th trump, but no side suit over five cards in length.

---

[13]Note that this part of *SCAMP* is not used as Responder, since trump is not known yet. This is further explained later in this chapter.

COUNT

Count is usually set at 20, since the bidder's side must amass at least 20 points in high cards during play of the hand or forfeit the bid (aces, tens and kings count as high cards). On this hand since we intend to take the bid, we must add at least 20. With a much stronger hand you may evaluate your *Count* as higher than 20.

ACES

Aces count is easy, since the bidder adds one point for each ace when holding at least four aces. For each ace over four, add 3 points. (Thus with five aces, you would add 7 points.) Likewise, one must deduct points when holding less than four aces. If holding only three aces, deduct 2 points. When holding only two aces, deduct 5 points. When holding only one ace, you should deduct 10 points and ask, *Why are you in the bidding*? In the previous hand you had to deduct 2 points since you held only three aces. If *Shape* and *Aces* combined equal less than –2, do not open the bidding in first or third hand position. Your hand is too weak.

MELD

Meld refers to the total meld held by the one making the bid. Of course, this includes the trump run if one is held and you intend to name the trump. The sample hand described above totals 65 points in meld, as you have a run[14] and a roundhouse for 35, plus 30 for double pinochle.

PARTNER

Partner has not bid on this hand, so expect no more than 10 points from partner, which may be a combination of aces and/or meld. This hand's evaluation for the bidder is 96.

---

[14]Note that when assessing your meld to send to your partner as Responder, you should not include any run, since at this point you have no way of knowing what suit your partner will name trump.

Using SCAMP as Declarer

Using the **SCAMP** Bidding System, we total up the points for the hand described previously, when bidding as the Declarer, or Opener:

Shape:	3 points
Count:	20 points
Aces:	–2 points
Meld:	65 points
Partner:	10 points

So, on this hand if you are the bidder and select spades as trump, you may bid at least up to 95. The rest of the hands (along with your own cards as South) are illustrated below.

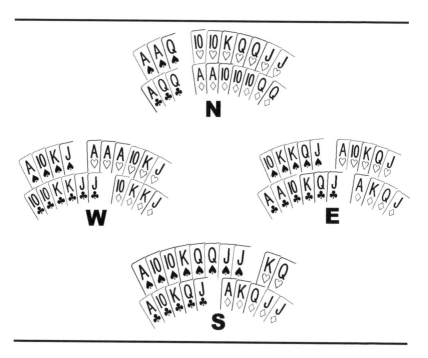

We have just described the major components of RAM's **SCAMP** Bidding System, when used by Declarer as bidder. *Shape, Count, Aces, Meld* and *Partner.*

Now we will learn how the Responder bids using this system. Consider the sample hand illustrated below:

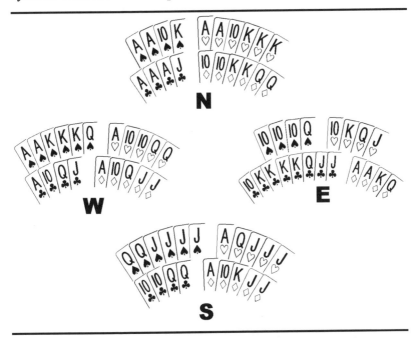

The table below[15] shows how bidding might progress.

EAST	SOUTH	WEST	NORTH
Pass	52	53	54
	Pass	Pass	Diamonds

East begins the bidding, and the last bid made was by North. After all others have passed, North declares diamonds as the trump suit after winning the bid. The process of using **SCAMP** for the example as shown is described below.

---

[15]A similar bidding table will be presented after each sample hand.

Responder only uses **A** and **M** of **SCAMP**, **A**ces and **M**eld. Count your total **Meld** and add 1 point for each of the first four aces. In addition, add 3 points for each ace you hold more than four. At the same time, you must deduct points when holding less than four aces. With only three aces, deduct 2 points, only two aces, deduct 5 points, only one ace, deduct 8 points. With no aces, deduct 11 points from your total.

SCAMP uses a one/over response [a bid just one more than the previous bid] to show 11-15 points and at least three aces when partner has bid in first position or second position.

Use this response to show more than the average 10 points partners usually count on. However, it is a hand not strong enough for a 20 jump. If your partner had opened the bidding and you had 4 aces along with 12 points or more you would send a 20 jump. But with only 3 aces you cannot count them as extra points. Be cautious of this response when partner opens in second position, since that bid may have been made only to save you as the dealer, and might not be a full opener.

South has 30 meld but deducts 5 points holding only two aces and so makes a 20 jump instead of 30. North seeing 30 meld on a 20 jump does not expect power from partner but intends to use his long hearts to force the opponent's trump out.

North opens with the double *Ace* and *King of Hearts*, holding back on his other aces until forced to play them. South wins and continues hearts. Each time North gets the lead, he pushes another round of hearts, the fifth and sixth round of hearts finally force everyone else to cut and expend their trump, effectively pulling trump for North. This earns a split of 25 HCP, added to their 38 meld for a total of 63 points.

Why We Developed a New Bidding System

I invented the **SCAMP** Bidding System to correct the woeful inadequacies of the old bidding methods in place for the last 150 years.

The old bidding method counted Meld, *Period*. Players were left to their own devices to estimate whether other features were strengths or weaknesses. Players had to be experts to factor in how much variables such as shape or distribution, number of aces, would add to or take away from the HCP score.

Unless you played with a set partner, it was hard to estimate exactly what a player was projecting when sending meld. Was it simply meld, or was strength factored in? Only play of the hand would tell. There would sometimes be a disparity of 15 to 45 percent between meld sent and the actual value of the hand. This often allowed opponents to steal the hand even when your team had equal meld or greater strength.

One of the best features of the **SCAMP** Bidding System is that your partner or the opponents do not have to be familiar with it. This is because the **SCAMP** Bidding System improves your *own* bidding skills while giving a more accurate picture of your hand. An obvious advantage over those not using it.

This advantage is doubled if you can get your partner to adopt it. But in any case, you have a decided enhancement over those opponents who are not using it. [*Especially if they are not even familiar with it. {!!}*]

Compare SCAMP with Standard Bidding

Did you notice some of the major differences between the old bidding methods and RAM's **SCAMP** Bidding System? As you review those listed below, it should give you added incentive to learn and apply this innovative bidding system. More details on employing it will be provided as you read on.

Lessons Learned:

In the boxes that follow, we will summarize some of the main differences between conventional bidding (usually showing meld only) and the **SCAMP** Bidding System as developed by RAM.

Can a player send an initial bid showing Aces?

Traditional Bidding	SCAMP
➢ Player only shows aces when holding one in each suit.	➢ Player shows aces, holding one in each suit, or when holding 10 or more meld and at least five aces in any suit, thus showing meld and aces at the same time.

Can a player show 12 - 15 points?

Traditional Bidding	SCAMP
➢ Player cannot show 12 to 15 points and must pass.	➢ If partner opens, show 12 to 15 points by making a one-over-one reply. You need at least three aces for this bid.

Can one show meld after bidding jumps to 60 or 65?

Traditional Bidding	SCAMP
➢ Player can show meld only when holding 30 or more Meld.	➢ A player shows meld and aces totaling over 20 by bidding one step over the last. Meld and aces totaling 30 or more are shown by jump bids. Jump of 10 shows 30, jump of 15 shows 40, a jump of 20 = 50 etc.

Can hand be evaluated accurately showing shape and distribution?

Traditional Bidding	SCAMP
➢ No standard values for shape or distribution. Player must make an estimation based on experience.	➢ Player can show distribution & shape using systemic values. Add 3 points for each trump over 7. Add 3 points for each card over five in a side suit.

Can one show meld and aces in the same bid?

Traditional Bidding	SCAMP
➢ Player shows meld only. Experts learn to shade meld up or down with the strength of their hand, but no standard exists that sets guidelines on what to expect, especially for newcomers.	➢ Player shows meld and adds points for aces when holding at least 4, and deducts points for holding less than 4 aces.

CHAPTER 3 - EVALUATING THE HAND
"One year from now, will you remember this hand?"

Why is it necessary to show values for shape and distribution? While meld and power [aces] are important factors in determining the number of tricks one can take, distribution also plays an important part in evaluating a hand. The more trump you have, the more tricks you are able to turn. This also is true of established side suits, so a value must be put on long side suits as well. It only remains then, to place a set value on long trump and side suits and establish it as a standard of reference.

The Value of Extra Trump

We have determined that a value of 3 for each trump over seven represents an accurate assessment of its trick-taking value. Likewise, appraising side suits, we found that a count of 3 for each card in a side suit over 5 accurately represents its value in producing HCPs.

How do we explain this concept in practical terms? Consider the following hand:

One can readily see that considering meld alone, this hand would be worth only 45 points. How much do you think the hand would pull in HCP?

Consider how we might play this hand. If you started off playing your high trump, you may take in about 11 points on the first five tricks. Play of the *Jack of Diamonds* may bring one additional point if partner wins with the *Ten*.

If you have been kind to elderly persons you may be rewarded with the *Ace of Hearts* at this point to make all the tricks. But maybe partner has no aces and returns the diamond suit like a good partner should. Your next five diamond tricks should bring in 13 points; the next three diamonds will add 7 points, as the opponents begin to run out of non-counters.

The next four trumps bring in 10 points. Give up the heart loser for 2 points and take the last trick for 48 HCP total.

So, the hand is worth not 45 points, but <u>93 points</u>! You assess the hand in advance by counting **Shape, Count, Aces, Meld & Partner. SCAMP** allows you to do this as a bidder.

Your **Shape** consists of ten trump, which is three over the minimum of seven. That gives you 3 points for each extra trump, (9 for **Shape.**) The **Count** we will leave at 20 for minimum HCP. **Aces** factored in gives you 4 points for the first four and 12 points for the next four (3 points for each ace over four.) **Meld** we already counted at 45. **Partner** did not bid, so how much you will play him for?

Just on your hand alone you add up the following; **Meld** 45, **Count** 20, **Shape** 9, **Aces** 16 for a total of 90 points. In effect, you have put a value of 45 on your hand play, estimating that you will make at least 45 HCP on your hand alone, not counting what your partner melds.

As seen from the play described above, you turned 48 points. You can readily see the accuracy of the **SCAMP** Bidding System. Please write me if you ever get the above hand and play it like that.

Let's see another example as applied to a more mundane bid such as the sample hand illustrated next.

Sample Hand 3a:

This hand would get a routine 51 bid from most players to show aces. This bid does not do justice to the true value of the hand. Some expert players upgrade the hand to show 20 meld in view of the aces. While still others bid 50, simply because they have a run.

The **SCAMP** Bidding System extracts the full worth of the hand by assessing it a 30 point jump bid after adding on points for the **Aces**.

How about the following hand with the new system?

Sample Hand 3b:

This hand counts 35 under the old biding method.

Under the **SCAMP** Bidding System we add on 10 for **Aces** and 6 for distribution [**Shape**], giving us 51 as the true value of the hand.

Any time accuracy is increased by 60%; one should sit up and take notice.

Better Bidding Usually Beats More Meld

Imagine the major swing involved in the next hand if North makes the 'business as usual' 51 bid, or even the more imaginative bid of 52. East would stomp them into a mud hole with 59 meld in his own hand. After he adds on the 10 he is expecting from partner, he's looking at 70 points before play.

No wonder East is up to 95 on this hand.

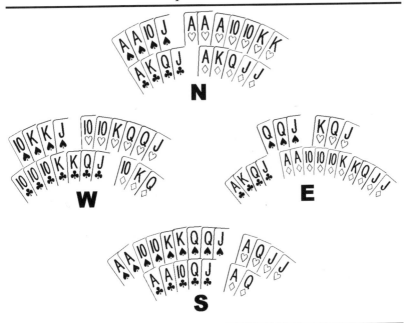

WEST	NORTH	EAST	SOUTH
Pass	53	75	85
	Pass	95	100
		Pass	Spades

North, however, uses the **SCAMP** Bidding System to make mush of the opposition with his 30 opening bid. South soars effortlessly to 100 and should make all 50 HCP.

Maybe I'm just a whiner, a complainer, a nitpicker or whatever. But it never fails to gall me when players fail to do the obvious, and jack up a perfect hand. What would stop two reasonably intelligent players from turning a Trickless[16] on this hand?

Once the trump are pulled and North sends back the *King of Hearts* for his partner, what in the world prevents South from stripping all the trump from the hand and returning to North in hearts for all the tricks? Maybe hands like these are what keep my hypertension up!

Lets look at another situation to analyze the accuracy of the **SCAMP** Bidding System. North opens with 51 bid, showing his whole hand on one bid, 10 meld with five aces.

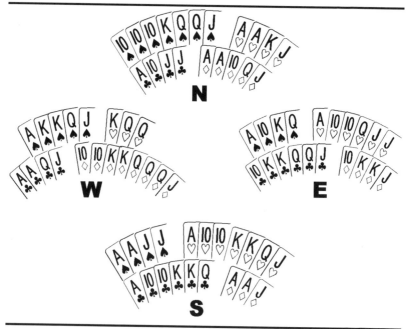

Look at how rapidly bidding concludes below:

NORTH	EAST	SOUTH	WEST
51	52	65	Pass
Pass	Pass	Hearts	

East thought about competing on his holding but South evaluates his hand at 70 points using Ram's **SCAMP** Bidding System.

SCAMP gives South a count of 3 points for **Shape**, since he has one card over five in a side suit while holding at least seven trumps. **Count**, gives him <u>20 points</u> (the HCP he must make for the save). **Aces** allows 1 point for each ace up to four and 3 points for each ace over four. Total 10 points. **Meld** of 27 points. **Partner** promises 10 points. South bids conservatively at 65, as he only wants to shut West out of the bidding. However we'd have no problem with a 70 bid at this point. With six aces and a promise of at least four aces from partner, he is also well fixed from a defensive position. East acquiesces.

Here's how the hand shown might play:

#	North	East	South	West
1	A♥	J♥	►Q♥ [17]	K♥
South sandbags aces {!}. (Defers playing aces to get the trump out first.) OK with an expert partner.				
2	►A♥	J♥	K♥	Q♥
North follows partner's lead in removing trump.				
3	►K♥	10♥	A♥	K♥

By refusing to play the *Ace of Hearts* at this first opportunity, East will gain an extra trump trick.

---

[17]The leader for each trick is shown in bold type and is preceded by an arrowhead (►). This convention will be followed throughout the book.

Watch continuation of play below:

#	North	East	South	West
4	J♥	10♥	▶K♥	K♦
5	J♣	▶Q♣	K♣	A♣
6	10♠	A♠	J♠	▶K♠
West's best play, looking for a 3 pointer.				
7	10♣	▶Q♣	A♣	J♣
8	J♣	K♣	▶Q♣	A♣
9	10♠	Q♠	A♠	▶K♠
East/West gets only 2 more tricks, aces in spades and hearts.				

North's 51 bid locked up the hand for South. More important, it showed South how the hand should be played to prevent the East/West save. Taking out trump first.

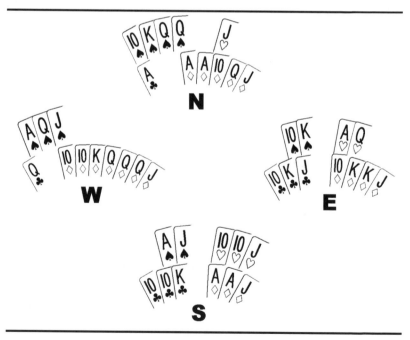

Since East/West have only 11 HCP at this point, they have not a prayer of saving their meld.

A Little Knowledge Can Go a Long Way

Once again, on the hand below we demonstrate the accuracy of RAM's **SCAMP** Bidding System. Under other bidding methods North would automatically pass this hand, South would compete and West would buy it at 65. East/West would then whine and console about how *"If you had just about anything partner, we woulda killed them."* They'd miss the bid by 8 points (no way North/South saves) and that would be that.

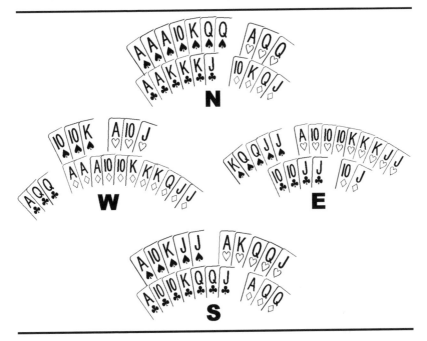

NORTH	EAST	SOUTH	WEST
52	Pass	60	65
Pass		70	Pass
		Clubs	

The Real Problem here? North/South had a super hand, but there would be no way for them to know the real strength of their combined hands using traditional bidding.

Using Ram's ***SCAMP*** Bidding System, what a difference! North counts 8 in ***Meld***, plus 4 for the first four aces and 3 each for the two aces over the fourth. That's 18, so he sends a 20 jump.

South counts up; 15 for the run, 10 for aces, 2 for the extra marriage totaling 27 for ***Meld.*** But, one point more for each of the four ***Aces*** gives a 31 total so far. Adding on the 20 from ***Partner*** gives us 51, plus 20 HCP for ***Count*** adds up to 71. No extra points for the ***Shape*** of this hand though.

See how much clearer the bidding becomes? Actually North/South make over 35 HCP on this hand because of the preponderance of aces.

RAM's ***SCAMP*** Bidding System can truly be termed revolutionary, as it overturns firmly entrenched standards and establishes fresh new criteria for both Openers and Responders to evaluate hands.

All who have examined ***SCAMP*** with an objective view have had to admit that it often fine tunes the final placement of a bid to within 3-5 points, as opposed to 5-15 points when compared to the conventional bidding methods used for the past 50 years.

Conventional Bidding	*SCAMP*
➢ High error in maximum bid (often 10 - 15 points or more) ➢ Usually 80% of bid estimate based on meld, no consistent use of other factors	➢ Much higher accuracy in bid (often within 3-5 points of hand) ➢ Only 40% of bidding estimate is based on meld, also uses other factors

Conclusion: Better bidding accuracy beats wishing for more meld, anytime.

"The Training Seat"

PART 2 - MODERN BIDDING METHODS

CHAPTER 4 - OPENER'S BIDS
"A Pinochle a day, keeps the psychiatrist away"

Observe the following hand and consider the bidding:

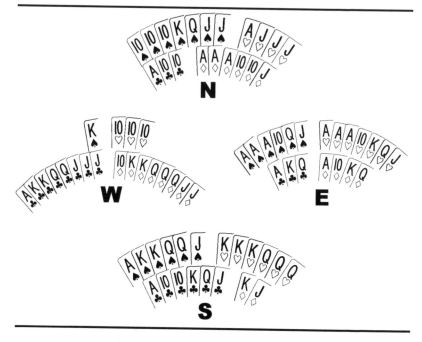

SOUTH	WEST	NORTH	EAST
52	Pass	53	54
60		Pass	65
Pass			Hearts

This South hand should not be opened in first position because of its **Shape** and lack of ace strength. With that measly six card club suit, South would be in danger of losing control right away if forced with repeated diamond ruffs.

Sending Meld as Declarer/Opener

We give South credit for not opening the hand, instead choosing to send meld, albeit reduced, to partner. North's perfunctory response showed no real interest in pursuing a career on this hand.

East was well endowed with power and felt safe in exploring options.

At this point perversity reared its head and prompted South to attempt a barricade bid with 60. East wonders what South will use for tricks.

East figured that with 35 **Meld** in hand, the possibility of assistance from **Partner**, and eight whipping sticks (**Aces**), there was no reason to sell out short. So East persisted to 65, which proved to be the final contract.

Ace of Clubs was led followed by the *Queen of Hearts*. This ran around to North, who cashed the *Ace of Clubs* and continued with the third club. South was in for the first time and brought clubs right back, East over-ruffing North's *Jack* with the *King of Hearts*.

East figured that with trump established, now would be a good time to go after the spades. Unfortunately West trumps in on the second round and for whatever reason, forces East with another club.

We expect the <u>opponents</u> to force Declarer to trump whenever possible and thus lose control of the hand, losing the bonus for last trick. That's their job!

Sometimes however, it's hard to imagine what thought processes would prompt your own partner to force you to trump in a situation like this. Be that as it may, it happens all the time.

East is now down to four trump and plays another spade trumped with West's last trump. Guess what he returns. Another club of course, reducing East to three trump.

East/West are able to salvage four of the last ten tricks for 26 HCP added to their 43 meld. If East/West had played their diamond losers early while they still had trump control, they would have prevented the North/South save.

With these cards left North/South add 24 HCP to their 40 meld to make an almost even hand, as shown with the remaining cards below.

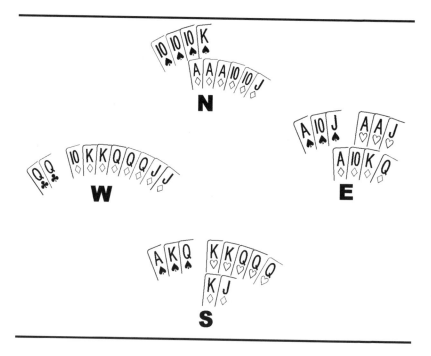

Counting up to Five

To learn the basics of the game, one only has to be able to count to five. However to become a good player, one must be willing to count to 20. In this book you will not only learn the basics, we will also show you how to count to 20 so that you can become good. That takes just a little more effort. Why is the count of five so important? Because the basic features of the game so often involve multiples of five. Take the unit known as the Sequence, or Run.

Imagine for a moment that you have selected spades as the trump suit. No doubt among your many spades you will have a run like this:

You see, it takes five cards to make a run. Look at your other spades:

Together they make a nice eight card suit, but only five of them count toward the run.

Here are the rest of your cards.

Add these twelve to your original eight and Voila! you become good overnight, because you counted up to 20. Each player is always dealt 20 cards, so let's analyze your 20. First we figure in your run, which would not be a run in another suit that is not trump. Since we intend to name the trump suit, we count spades as trump.

Be Sure to Count Those Other Fifteen

Let's see how many Meld combinations we can get from your whole hand. To do this we must refer to the Meld Chart in the Appendix or back in *Chapter 2* if you prefer.

- The run by itself counts for 15 points, but combined with a roundhouse [a king and queen in each suit] counts for 35 points.
- An ace in each suit makes 10 more points.
- Jacks in each suit for 4 points and a pinochle, [*Jack of Diamonds* plus *Queen of Spades*] for 4 points more.

So total it up, run and roundhouse together counts 35, plus 10 for aces around equals 45, jacks around and pinochle add 8; totals 53 **Meld**. Your partner contributes 14 **Meld**, which gives the partnership Total **Meld** of 67. Oh! Did you forget to add in the 4 points for the four aces, and 3 more points for the fifth ace giving you 7 total for **Aces**?

While we're at it, remember your **Shape**, your eighth spade counts for 3. That boosts your total to 77 and means you can bid as high as 95 without feeling stressed.

Maybe you got the bid for only 65, but you still need 20 HCP to make your bid. [There's that 20 again.] You see now that it takes no skill to pick up melds (some pick up an inordinate amount). But we must be more than good, to get our 20 HCP. We must be better.

Let's see how the bidding might have proceeded on this hand. Perhaps your partner was the dealer and your Right Hand Opponent (RHO) opened the bidding with 50. Your hand has support for all the suits and a suit of your own.

The first thing to do is let your partner know the strength of your hand. *Meld* counts the roundhouse for 24, aces for 10, jacks and pinochle for 8 plus your **Aces** power of 4 points plus 3, for 7 total points there. That adds up to 49 for *Meld*.

We can't count your run at this time because you are sending meld to your partner and you don't know what suit will eventually end up as trump. You remember it's only a run if your sequence turns out to be the suit that's made trump.[18] Anyway, you probably can't count on your partner making spades trump.

Now your figure of 49 must be communicated to your partner. For meld around the 20 mark (16-25) we make a jump of **two**, for meld around 30 (26-35), we jump by **three**, but your meld is almost 50, so how far must we jump?

Yes, **five** is the number. We must jump the bidding by **five** points to let partner know we have 50 *Meld* for him. Since the bidding is now at 50, a jump of **five** will bring you to what number? Exactly, <u>55.</u> That is the bid you must make to inform your partner of your support. Suppose the bid was already up to 53. What bid would you have to make, to jump **five** points? Well, 53 plus 5 is <u>58</u>. That bid also would tell your partner that you hold around 50 points.

Any jump of **five** over the last bid shows 50 meld. So, you bid 55, your LHO bids 56 and your partner passes, obviously not able to take the bid even with your 50 points. RHO now bids 60.

---

[18]You will recall that this is also the reason that you cannot send anything about the Shape of your hand as Responder since that also depends on trump.

What do these bids mean? First the RHO bids 50 to say: *"Partner I have a suit and would like to take this bid; do you have any meld for me?"*

Then your bid 55: *"Partner, I have 50 points for you if you want to take this bid."*

Next the LHO bids 56: *"Partner I do not have as much as 20 meld to send you, but I do have a suit of my own that I like pretty good."*

Your Partner, Pass: *"Sorry, I have no decent suit to bid in myself, and not as much as 20 meld to send you."*

RHO bids 60: *"Well, I'll just take the bull by the horns and try to grab this bid myself."*

Now it's your turn again.

Remember that your hand rises in value if spades are trump because of the run that gives you 53 in meld, plus your 10 points for **Aces** power and **Shape**. Add that to the 20 you must make in HCP, for 83.

I know since I explained the numbers to you, you won't let anybody take this bid from you for less than 85, so you bid 65 this time and all pass. Your partner contributes 14 points and you are now at the point where you can play the hand.

But we won't play it out this time, because we can't see what the other players had.

Should You Open the Bidding with a Weak Hand?

Moving right along...let's see what could happen when you choose to open light (bid with a weak hand) in the first position. Most experts tend to avoid opening very light hands in first position. This South hand proves why this is so. After overbidding partner twice, South seized the advantage of a 60 bid and was rewarded by all he could possibly expect from his partner.

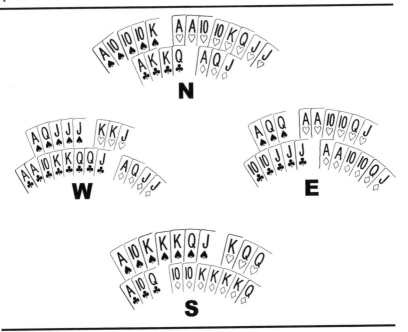

SOUTH	WEST	NORTH	EAST
50	51	52	Pass
53	54	55	
56	57	Pass	
60	Pass		
Spades			

How will South salvage this weak hand with a plus score, needing 23 HCP to make the bid?

South starts by cashing the *Ace of Clubs* and leads the *Queen of Trump* [♠] forcing West to play the *Ace of Spades*. West plays two *Club Aces* and a low club to get South cutting early. South next tries the *King of Spades*.

North has the stage and cashes two *Heart Aces*, the *Ace of Diamonds* and exits with a low heart.

East wins with the *Ten of Hearts*, cashes the *Ace of Trump* [♠] and makes South cut the fifth club, pulling South's *King* and North's *Ten of Spades* in the process.

North further contributes to the debacle making partner use up trumps by leading another small heart pulling South's *Ten of Trump* [♠]. South finally decides to get rid of some losers and exits with the *Queen of Diamonds*.

West is now on lead with the *Ace of Diamonds* and returns the *Queen of Clubs*, which removes all remaining trump and reduces the hand to a shambles.

North/South end up with the minimum 20 HCP. Too bad they really needed 23!

Looking at South's hand in retrospect, it doesn't seem worthy of so many bids. Perhaps a Pass would be advisable after North bids the second time.

In all fairness, if South opens with his long losing suit, playing the *Queen of Diamonds* instead of his *Ace of Clubs*, he gains the advantage of timing. In that case the hand is unbeatable under any defense.

But like they say, *"If you bid Big, Ya gotta play Big!"*

Opening Bidding in First and Third Position

Many seasoned players fail to appreciate the incentives offered by the first and third hand positions at the table. The two main advantages are Timing and Choice. We will consider each of these factors as they influence the bidding for players in the first and third hand position. The player bidding first, is in position to take the bid, send meld, or to convey strength with relatively little risk.

That's why RAM's **SCAMP** Bidding System advocates use of the 51 bid in first position to show at least five aces and 6 to 10 meld points. This opens up a range heretofore untapped by the old standard bidding.

Previously, if one did not have an ace in each suit, there was no way to show this wide swath of power. Actually, it should have been obvious by sheer weight of numbers. Five aces compared to four aces is an increase of 20 percent. If I promise you four or more aces with 10 meld, then my meld reveals me to have five or more aces with 10 meld or more, is that not an added value that should be appreciated?

Some diehards argue: *"I don't like it, I wanna Know where the aces are!"* True, you may not know exactly what suit each ace is in, but suppose partner passed with the 10 points and five aces; how much would you know then? At least now, you know his point range and that aces are there, you've only got to locate them. All this information you did not know initially.

So, the first position allows one this flexibility that is often lost in the second position. This timing advantage also extends itself to showing meld. Since meld in the first position is sent before anyone else has had an opportunity to bid, an additional benefit accrues to your partner. Your partner in the third hand position, is often now able to place the final contract before fourth hand has even entered the bidding.

In the bidding sequence below, East's bid will often close the bidding, since 65 may have been as high as fourth hand could stretch:

WEST	NORTH	EAST	SOUTH
52	54	65	?

Hands such as the following examples lend themselves to such a progression;

Sample Hand 4a:

With this East hand we would bid 65 or 70 after a 20 meld bid from partner. Why? For **Shape** you would count 3 points for the eighth trump, 3 points for the sixth heart, and 3 points for the sixth club. Add on 20 points for **Count**, and 20 for **Meld**. This totals 49 but I know you will subtract 2 points for the fact that you have only three **Aces**. Adding this 47 to Partners meld of 20 gives you 67.

Actually, if partner's values are in the right places, this hand could very well make 75 or 80 instead of 65. For example, if partner has the *Ace of Spades, Ace of Hearts* and two *Club Aces* along with his 20 meld, the hand will make lots more. If instead, he has all four *Diamond Aces,* aces in that suit would have no value for you since you are void in diamonds. We call this wasted values.

Sample Hand 4b:

K J J J ♠ A 10 K Q Q J J ♡ A K J ♣ A A 10 10 K J ♢

Here you should bid 70 or 75 after partner sends 20 meld. You have only seven trumps [♥], but add on 3 in **Shape** for the sixth diamond. Add on 20 for **Count,** 4 for your four **Aces,** and 27 for **Meld,** totaling 54. Your partner's 20 meld takes you to 74.

Sample Hand 4c:

A 10 K J ♠ 10 10 K K K Q J ♡ A A 10 K Q Q J ♣ K J ♢

A typical 70 bid after partner sends 20 meld. This time, you count 6 points in **Shape** for your sixth and seventh hearts. Add your 29 **Meld** to 20 **Count,** subtract 2 for having only three **Aces.** That's 53 and partner's 20 meld makes 73 points total. Get your 70 bid in, before the others get wise to you.

Sample Hand 4d:

Q J J ♠ A A ♡ A K K J J J ♣ A A 10 10 K Q Q Q J ♢

This hand in the **SCAMP** Bidding System counts 53. **Shape,** 9, (3 each for the eighth and ninth trump and 3 for the sixth club.) 20 for **Count,** 7 for **Aces,** and 19 for **Meld.** With 20 meld from **Partner,** bid 75!

Making closeout bids like these often takes opponents out of the bidding, once you have placed the contract as high as you deem it possible for you to make.

What then, if one hears bidding like the following?

WEST	NORTH	EAST	SOUTH
52	54	65	70
Pass	Pass	75?	

Something is wrong with this picture. Was East originally placing the contract as high as possible? If East was saying on the first bid, *"This is as high as I can go!"* then what is he saying now?

Maybe, *"I'm 10 points higher than I can make and will certainly go set at this level."* Perhaps East hopes South will overbid, go on to 80 [and go set hopefully?]

We mentioned two advantages in first position. One was choice? One has a choice when bidding first. One is not required to volunteer any information in first position.

Our partner in the third seat is likewise devoid of any burden to get involved in the bidding without just cause. It can always be left to the dealer who may indeed be the player with the most power, but no meld.

If no intervening bids have occurred by the time the bidding has reached the third position, perhaps a mediocre hand is not one to test the waters with. Such a hand might best be left to the dealer's devices to figure out. Especially so when third hand finds less than four aces in a hand blessed at the same time with double pinochle or roundhouse and an even hand.

Where is the Power? Your partner in first position showed no aces, so where are you going with this hand? What are you going to use for tricks? Surely discretion here would prove to be the better part of valor. If you have no power, why save the dealer? Let him find his own way out of the forest, (if he can find the cookie crumb trail).

Opening Bids in Fourth Hand Position

Is there a difference when opening the bidding in fourth hand? Remember that the dealer must take the bid if 3 hands pass. However, the dealer does NOT have to play the hand. The dealer may choose to throw in the hand [without consultation with partner] and go set for 50 points. In this case the opponents do not get to meld because no trump was named.[19]

On the other hand, the dealer may choose to name a trump and play the hand. This allows the opponents to meld and make a positive score, which would be denied them if the hand was thrown in. What then, should be the standard that governs whether to play or throw it in?

The basic rule should be for you to have at least enough meld to get down yourself (20 meld) without your partner, and you should have at least your average share of the aces (three or four). If your partner has 10 points you will be in the ballpark.

If you don't have these basic requirements, you may want to cut your losses, throw in the hand and get on to the next deal. Don't prolong your misery unnecessarily.

What is the reasoning here?

If your partner could not scrape up a bid knowing you were the dealer with the possibility of getting stuck, where will he get the points to help you make your minimum 20 meld?

The following are examples of hands you might hold and what you may consider, if you take the bid at 50, or just decide to throw it in and cut your losses.

---

[19]When playing in some localities, such as the NPA, or Yahoo! on the Internet, after three passes the dealer <u>must</u> name a suit if holding a marriage. So, always check the rules before you start the game.

Sample Hand 4e:

Go for it! You have 29 points in **Meld** alone (and even when you subtract 2 points for only having three **Aces** you still have 27 points.) If your partner has as much as 2 meld (just a plain marriage will do here,) you only need the 20 HCP minimum to make your bid.

Sample Hand 4f:

Don't even think about it! The **SCAMP**. Bidding System makes this one a no-brainer.

With 6 points and five aces your partner would open the bidding with 51 (if you're playing **SCAMP.**) Let's be generous and give him 8 points and four aces, to make the partnership total of 23 points and seven aces at best. Now you need 27 HCP with less than half of the aces, one ace in your lame trump suit and no side suit you can establish. What are your chances of pulling 27? So you're going 'bete' if you bid. Meanwhile, the opponents will meld 20-30 or whatever, plus at least half of the HCP for a 50-point gain added to minus 50. All of a sudden they're a hundred ahead. That's what we mean by '*cut your losses*'. Take your minus 50 set and move on to the next hand. They get nothing extra when you throw the hand in.

Are you still curious about the other hands around the table?

Here's one sample *(remember you hold the South hand)*:

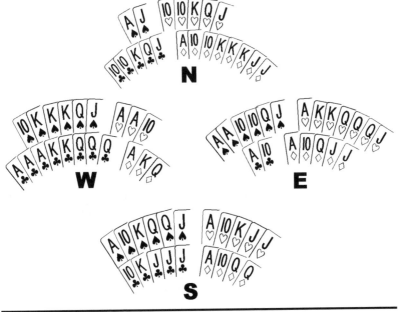

Here's another sample *(you are still South below)*:

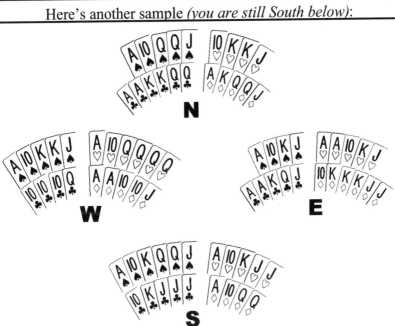

And one more for emphasis:

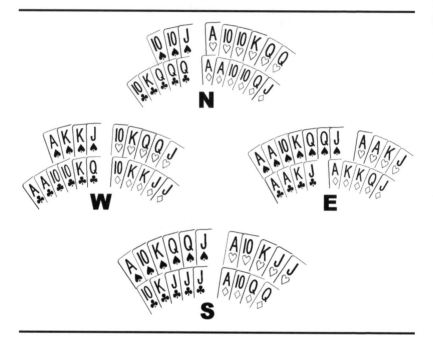

If none of those partner hands impressed you, that's good, now you know what to expect in those cases.

What about other mediocre hands such as shown below?

Sample Hand 4g:

This one is a So-So. Just remember that of the three available hands out there, your partner probably has the worst.

Your LHO may have a strong hand but no suit, so he passed. Your RHO probably has meld and power but no long strong suit, so took a chance to see if you would come in his suit where he has triple aces but no marriage (*yes, that's diamonds.*) Your partner couldn't send 20 meld, not even 10 meld with aces, and lastly, knowing you dealt, could not even bid zero [*50.*] Where are you going with your flat featureless hand, so much better suited for support?

What could you expect to find out there? Hey! Your partner has the max on this one,

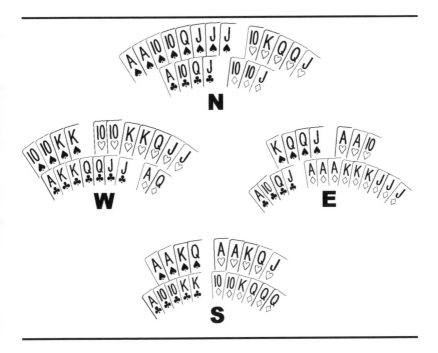

Maybe by scraping nails, biting teeth and tenacious clawing, you might be able to lock in enough points to make it. Not convinced yet? Another sample?

Okay, look at this one:

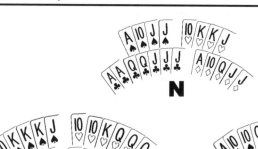

And a final example:

These samples depict real life and are intended to show what to expect on average, if partner passes in second position.

One more tip. In fourth position, after your partner has passed and you decide to throw the hand in, don't ask what your partner had. It's bad form, and it won't help you. In fact, it may weaken your resolve to do the right thing the next three times this situation comes up. That may be the time when partner has even less. If you made the right decision for the average hand, don't torment yourself with what might have been.

What about the other hands that follow?

Sample Hand 4h:

K K K Q Q Q J ♠   A A A J ♡   A A Q J ♣   10 10 K Q J ♢

Full speed ahead! It's time to take a chance. You have a seven card suit (albeit flawed) slightly more than your share of the aces, five, and you can get yourself on the board with 22 meld. With 6 or 8 points from your partner along with three or four aces you will do nicely, thank you very much.

Sample Hand 4i:

A 10 K Q Q J ♠   K Q Q J ♡   10 10 Q J ♣   10 10 10 Q Q J ♢

Now here's a doozy! You certainly have more than enough to get down, all you need is a save. What would your partner need to hold in order for you to save?

I think we would do better to allow you to figure this one out. Personally, I would rely on my knowledge of the opponents. Yes, I'd Play the Players! If I recognized their defensive skills as exceptional so far, I'd tend to throw it in. However, if they haven't yet shown me they're worthy of respect, I might take a chance.

Sample Hand 4j:

All Systems Go! You have 29 meld, your share of the aces, and a six card suit that you should not be too proud of, but Hey, you were never promised a rose garden. Such is the spice of life, when you can tell your grandchildren; *"I remember the time I opened this hand with only..."*

What might solidify your thinking on this is to deal three or four sample hands in the following manner:

- Take your hand out of the deck then deal out three other hands.
- Select as your partner's hand, the one that could not send meld or open.
- See if the two of you have enough to make 20-25 HCP.

Repeat as needed until you see what the averages show. Let that be your future guide.

For those of you who have a mandatory play rule for the dealer, these tips do not apply. If you as the dealer have no choice about whether or not to play the hand, then of course you must lay down whatever you have and hope for the best.

For historical perspective, we have unearthed the fossilized remainder of a hand from the early Jurassic period:

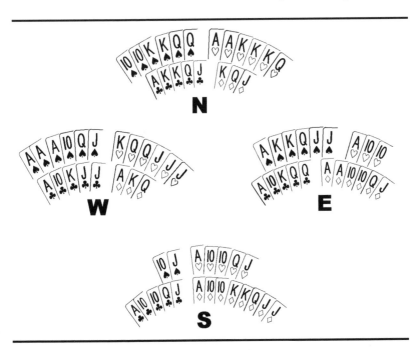

SOUTH	WEST	NORTH	EAST
50	Pass	52	60
65		Pass	Pass
Diamonds			

South chose to open with a substandard hand in first position. The South hand would be opened if you were in second position since the dealer might have significant meld but no suit to bid. However, in first position it's a crapshoot, hoping that partner has specifically, *meld* **and** *power*.

Fortunately for South, partner has three aces. With little more than half of the outstanding trumps, North/South are not without some anxious moments.

By the skin of their teeth, they are able to pull the 20 HCP needed to save this bid. Watch how:

#	North	East	South	West
1	K♥	10♥	▶A♥	J♥
2	K♣	Q♣	▶A♣	J♣
3	J♦	10♦	▶Q♦	K♦
W. {!} Allows partner who melded aces, to get in.				
4	Q♥	▶A♥	J♥	K♥
5	Q♠	▶A♠	J♠	A♠
W. Plays Ace-on-Ace! (Means keep playing the suit!)				
6	Q♠	▶K♠	10♠	A♠
7	K♠	J♠	K♦	▶10♠
After seven tricks, N/S have 8 of the 20 HCP they need.				
8	A♣	Q♣	▶Q♣	K♣
9	▶K♦	A♦	J♦	Q♦
10	K♠	▶J♠	K♦	J♠
11	J♣	A♣	▶J♣	10♣
12	Q♦	▶J♦	10♦	A♦
E. {!} Good Play, takes away one of South's points.				
13	10♠	Q♠	10♦	▶Q♠

North/South have 14 points now and there's no way to stop them from another 6. Again, by hocking the family jewels, North/South are able to pull the 20 HCP needed to save this bid.

This chapter should help you to see the dynamics going on, once the bidding has passed to the fourth seat. By extension, you should also know how to jam a fellow player in the fourth seat. [*Did I say that?*] Oh My! I must adjust my thinking to reflect a more charitable character. [*Perhaps in my next book?*]

"The Weekly Treat"

CHAPTER 5 - RESPONDER'S BIDS
*"Pinochle is not a matter of Life or Death,
It's much more serious than that"*

Whenever your partner has opened the bidding in first or third position, there are only three bids available to you. You may Pass (sometimes the safest bid,) you may Overcall (bid the next number,) or you may Jump the bidding. We'll examine each of these options carefully, since this is often where the hackers, are separated from the Real Players.

Hey, You Can Always Pass

Never underestimate the value of a pass. Remember that your partner will usually play you to have an average of 10 points and three or four aces in your hand, even when you pass. If you choose to make a forward going bid, he will expect more because after all, you could have passed. Many players after their partner opens the bidding, feel they must bid their hand (show a new suit.) Wrong!

Your partner has opened the bidding showing a good suit she wants to make trump. Why does she need to hear about another suit? There's no way to make two suits trump! So unless you have at least a nine card run with double ace or better, there's no need to bid just to show a suit after your partner has opened the bidding, she already HAS a suit. *Once again, if your partner opens the bidding, or overcalls when the opponents bid, your next bid should usually show MELD.*

Usually you should show meld with minimum values as a Responder. What do you do with a hand like the following?

| A K | A 10 K K Q Q | 10 10 K K Q J | A 10 10 K Q J |
| ♠ ♠ | ♡ ♡ ♡ ♡ ♡ ♡ | ♣ ♣ ♣ ♣ ♣ ♣ | ♢ ♢ ♢ ♢ ♢ ♢ |

Give a 20-meld bid after partner opens. Maybe he will hit one of your six-card suits. If not, you still have 16 points and three aces. That certainly merits a 20 bid. If you have at least three aces and 12 to 15 points you could bid one over the last number bid. Again, this should show support for your partner's bid, not a suit of your own, unless you bid a second time.

How High Should I Jump Bid?

Anytime the bidding is jumped, skipping over a level; there is a significant reason for it. We call this a Jump bid. Jump bids by a Responder normally have only one purpose, to show the Responder's partner what **Aces** and **Meld** to expect.

In short, to show the total of **Aces** and **Meld,** you should jump the bidding by 10% of the amount you hold. This is rather simple when the bidding is between 50 and 58. If your **Aces** and **Meld** total is 12 -15, that's in the 10 range, no need to jump, just bid 1 over. [That's 10% of 10.] If your **Aces** and **Meld** total 17-25, that's the 20 range, so you jump the bidding by 2 over the last bid. If your **Aces** and **Meld** fall in the 30 range (26 to 35) jump the bidding by 3. For the 40 range 36 to 45, jump by 4. With 46 to 55 jump by 5. A jump of 6 would show 56 to 65, and so on.

One specialized bid is reserved for double aces only. It is the bid of 59. Anytime you jump the bidding from any point to 59; partner will be looking for you to have specifically, double aces in each suit. If your partner jumps the bidding to 59 and the next player passes, if you have a marriage, ***Don't Even Think About Passing!*** Your partner may not have a marriage and be forced to throw the hand in. Remember, you must have a marriage to take the bid and make trump.

On auctions when partner opens in first position, or overcalls (one-over-one) in second position, the opponents may take up your space for showing meld by bidding 60 or 65. Now it is no longer possible to show meld in the usual manner.

In that case, if your **Aces** and **Meld** are in the 20 range you may not be able to send it. If your range however, puts you in the 30 bracket, you may respond with a jump of 10 to show thirty or more. A jump of 15 will show 40 points, a jump of 20 shows 50 and so on. This prevents you from being shut out of the bidding, or pre-empted when your side has the good stuff.

Players in the NPA or using the Florida System will often make openings of 60 or 65. to prevent the opponents from throwing meld. Ram's **SCAMP** Bidding System has a built-in response for this. If your partner opens first hand, or overcalls in second position, you can show a full opening bid by making a simple overcall after an opponent's preemptive bid. By full opening, we mean 20+ points and three or more aces. In that case, the bidding might proceed:

Bidding Sample 5a:

SOUTH	WEST	**YOU**	EAST
50	60	65	?

Bidding Sample 5b:

SOUTH	WEST	NORTH	**YOU**
50	51	60	65

Bidding Sample 5c:

SOUTH	WEST	**YOU**	EAST
50	65	70	?

Since you will not be bidding just to show a suit after your partner opens, each of these sample bids should show a full opening bid with support for your partner. *5C* must be a tad stronger, since you are forcing your partner up to the 75 level.

Here is a Responder jump after a preemptive bid.

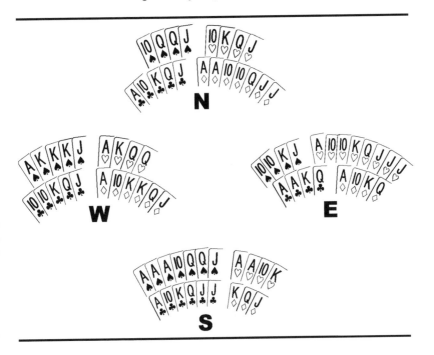

EAST	SOUTH	WEST	NORTH
52	53	70	85
Pass	90	Pass	Pass
	Clubs		

West tried to disrupt dialogue by bidding what he thought he could make on this hand. North properly sent his values by jumping 15, showing 40 points. South bids 90 and is rewarded with the added bonus that partner has a run in his suit.

Often players differ as to whether you should send meld to a partner when you intend to take the bid yourself. We subscribe to the quaint notion that all-else being equal; partnership spirit is best served by sending the meld first. Of course, there are occasions you must shut out both opponents and partner. In such cases we hope partner will be forgiving.

Scaling Down Jump Bids on Weak Hands

North sent meld on this hand but scaled it down to 30, because the hand was so weak.

Anytime you receive a 30 meld bid and observe 42 meld come down on the board, Look Out! You are forewarned to look elsewhere for playing tricks, since partner is probably flat broke on aces. On the following sample North sent the weak meld and ended up with the bid.

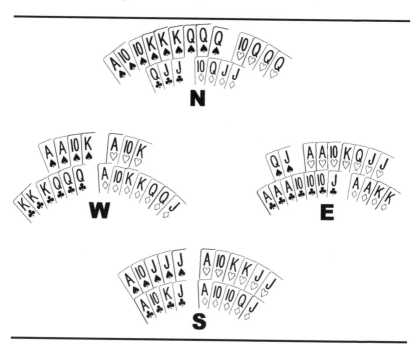

NORTH	EAST	SOUTH	WEST
53	54	Pass	56
60	65		Pass
70	Pass		
Spades			

South, without a marriage, could not name a suit. But playing **SCAMP**, South could send a 20 jump bid to show 14 *Meld* and four **Aces,** giving North less of a problem.

Fortunately, in this auction North was not inclined to give up the hand halfheartedly and needed no encouragement to persist to 70. With 48 points in meld, North was not looking for points from partner. Just a couple of aces, Please! North's pulse slows down visibly, as South lays four 'sticks' (*aces*) on the table assuring the save even with the best defense.

East/West can't be denied their save, but North/South's 62 points don't go down the drain. This would be inevitable if the opponents got the bid in their suit.

How Much is Enough?

The next hand illustrates the need to give up as much information as quickly as possible.

This principle might be expressed in the question *"How many chances will I have to tell my partner anything about my hand?"*

Usually only one. After that you will be passing.

Let's try **SCAMP** bidding on this next hand:

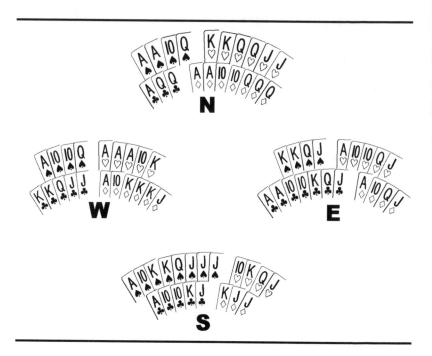

WEST	NORTH	EAST	SOUTH
51	Pass	65	Pass
Pass		Clubs	

West wanted to get a message to partner quickly, and sent a bid of 51. We said that an opening bid of 51 is reserved for hands of 6-13 points with at least one ace in each suit. However, many advanced players use this bid even without aces in every suit, when they hold at least five aces in total.

West's hand, had the required five aces but no suit to bid, so 51 was a good bid. We recommend the use of this bid with 6-13 points because when 4 points for the first four aces are added in, plus 3 points for the fifth ace, you still show more than 10 points.

If you have as much as 14 HCP with four or more aces, we recommend that you show 20 meld since the 4-7 point bonus still puts you in the 20 point range.

North with 10 points but no biddable suit was shut out, leaving East free to romp to 65. Note that had West passed, North could make the same 51 bid, allowing South to bring in the spade suit for 65. If truth be told, most hands fall in this average category, with either side able to make 60 to 65 in their own suit. So, the side finding out the most about the hand first, naturally, has the advantage.

The play of this hand carried no surprises. East's *Queen of Trump* [♣] opening ran up to North's *Ace*.

North played double *Ace of Spades* continuing with the *Ten*. South played the *Ace of Spades* and returned spades.

West won and played the *Ace of Diamonds*. The *Queen of Clubs* pushed the *Ten* to South's *Ace*. A small spade was then led and won, East over-ruffing West's *King* with the *Ten of Clubs*. Next, East played the *Ace of Diamonds* and led back the *Jack* around to North's *Ace of Diamonds*.

North returned the *King of Hearts* which East won with the *Ace*. East led the *Queen of Diamonds* trumped by South with the *Ten of Clubs*. South served up one more *Spade* trumped by West and East with the *King* and *Ace of Clubs*.

East gave up the *Jack of Clubs* to South's *Ten* for North/South's last trick to save 20 points on the nose.

Reading Meld after Jump Bids

Sometimes Responder is forced to lie about points but all becomes apparent when the meld is revealed.

Notice this in the following hand:

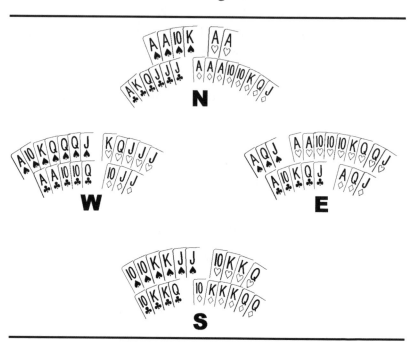

SOUTH	WEST	NORTH	EAST
57	58	60	65
Pass	75	80	95
	Pass	100	Pass
		Diamonds	

South's hand though rich in meld, is dreadfully weak as a trick taker. That's why even with 88 meld, the maximum deduction of 12 points is made for an ace-less hand.

West makes a temporizing bid of 58. A bid of 59 would show double aces, while 60 would indicate a desire to take the bid. The bid will be clarified on the next round if partner can enter the auction.

North waits at 60 (not really worried, since partner sent 70 meld, I guess you can afford to fool around.) Personally, I see no need to let the opponents muck about in the auction, so I probably would have bid 70 here to discourage sharing.

East of course makes a bid here with 41 meld.

West comes up strong with a 10 jump showing 30 or more meld. East intends to take this hand to the Max. With nine trump, aces, and partner sending a belated 30, 100 points might be in the ballpark. However it is not to be this time.

North, holding eight aces, is prepared to go to the moon, (with or without a capsule.) When North sees all that meld, its obvious that no power will come out of partners hand.

So, the proper way to play this hand is to cash out the side suit aces and let partner throw points. Then we push the club suit. Eventually South will get two ruffs. North/South lose only two spades, three clubs and a trump for 160+ total points.

Even with eight aces East/West cannot save their meld as their trump [♦] holding proves to be woefully inadequate.

Good thing East, who was keeping the score, wrote their meld down lightly, so it's not too hard to erase.

Jump Bids Don't Always Show Meld

Two jump bids by Responders make the next hand worthy of consideration. Take a look:

N

W

E

S

WEST	NORTH	EAST	SOUTH
51	52	60	75
Pass	80	Pass	Pass
	Spades		

The first jump bid by West promises at least 10 points in aces and meld, showing either an ace in each suit or a minimum of five aces. This bid can only be made when you are first to open the bidding. Although this bid is made first, we still class it as a Responder's bid because it is made with the anticipation of partner taking the bid.

North's bid of one-over is a waiting bid to see if partner can send meld.

East's jump bid to 60 is not a meld bid since he had an opportunity to send meld at any level between 52 and 59. His bid simply shows he is prepared to take the helm and name the contract.

The next bid by South is a Responder's jump bid showing meld. Since this is South's first chance to show meld, South jumps the bidding by 15 to show 40 meld points. North has no problem in recognizing it as a meld bid and takes the bid at 80 as shown.

This is another Stevie Wonder hand (even a blind man could play it.) The *Ace of Diamonds* first, then the longest side suit in hopes that anybody will trump in and use up their trumps in this manner.

With proper defense East/West will save their meld.

The only way to stop them would be the highly unusual *Ten of Clubs* lead from the North hand at trick two or trick five. This reaches South, who can then pick up the diamond losers, at the same time exposing North as a shameless cheater.

Of course, under no circumstances would you pass a jump meld bid if you have a biddable suit. Partner may not have a trump marriage, or his marriage may be in a three or four card suit.

Ignoring a jump bid of this type is one of the quickest ways to dissolve a partnership, or cause your own marriage to lose its flavor. Either that, or maybe you will be encouraging your partner into the bad habit that is discussed next.

Hiding Meld From Your Partner

Responders have another nasty habit, which we will touch on briefly here. They become very secretive about some holdings and decide to hide them. Yes, concealing meld is a well known habit among Pinochle players the world over, though at times it is hard to define it's merits. Who are you concealing the meld from, and why? Certainly not the opponents, they could care less how much meld you have, or lose, as long as they are able to grab the bid and get their suit named. Actually, they would prefer that you have more meld than you knew about. So who's being fooled the most? As usual, it's your partner, the one you vowed to support in sickness and health.

You're most likely hiding the meld from the one who stands to benefit most from your meld. What's the favorite excuse of the meld hiders? *"Sorry, but I wanted the bid partner."* So what? Does sending your meld prevent you from wanting the bid? I think not, surely you are in position to bid again. And what makes you think from an examination of your hand only, your partner not yet heard from, that you know all that needs to be known about this hand?

Maybe your partner has a trump suit like the following:

But he has no other meld. And there you are, sitting on a double pinochle, kings and three marriages with a run. Oh, did I mention that you're missing two aces and two tens in your trump? Meanwhile, you won't send the meld because *'you like your hand'*? These kinds of things make people want to play with somebody else. Anybody else! OK that's off my chest.

So Send Partner Your Meld

In this hand South does send meld even with a nice suit of his own. North has more distributional values with a three suiter (three points for each card in a side suit over five). As it happens, North/South has found a good fit in the spade suit.

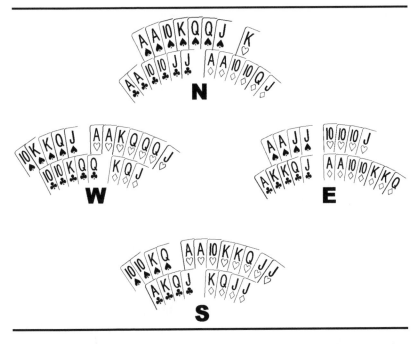

EAST	SOUTH	WEST	NORTH
51	54	56	60
Pass	65	Pass	70
	Pass		Spades

As often happens, the opening lead of the *Queen of Trump* [♠] from the North hand clears up a multitude of sins.

East has no way to get past the South hand, over to his partner. As a result, East/West are unable to save anything on this deal.

"Setting the Record Straight"

Sometimes you wonder how you would have made it without your partner's help. Then there are hands you wonder how you manage **with** your partner's help.

Don't make your partner want to get along without you!

Interpreting Responder's Jump Bids

Since a jump bid is what you always <u>want</u> to hear, it is often deceptive when not interpreted properly. On the next hand we class South as a Responder. Why?

It is not South's intention at this point to take the bid. South may be forced to take the bid if North passes, but the original intent is to send meld. That is why we call South a Responder. Note that South has jumped the bidding by **four** points, what does this mean?

Well, let's count the assets. There's a double pinochle for 30 points, a double marriage in spades for 4 points, another 4 points for each ace up to four, for a total of 38 points. That's in the 40 range and a jump bid of **four** should show it.

What happens when partner counts up the meld and finds that South has only 34 points in meld? It means that there must be aces along with this bid, at least four, possibly more.

What do you lead when you and your partner have aces? I guess it depends on whether or not you want the opponents to cut your aces. If you don't want your aces cut, you should try to take out the opponent's trumps, first.

But you say, *"North's trumps are rather weak."* All the more reason to try to get them out. You don't want an opponent sitting over you at the end with your top trumps. You could lose the last trick bonus. So when it's *'Pay Me Now, or Pay Me Later'* pay them Now, not Later!

Look at the example shown below:

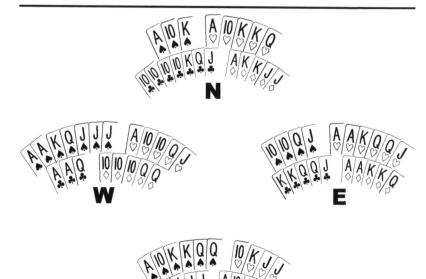

SOUTH	WEST	NORTH	EAST
54	Pass	55	Pass
Pass		Clubs	

First things first, of course. You have an *Ace of Spades* hanging that you could lose, so you play it first, then the *Queen of Trumps* [♣]. South plays double *Ace of Trumps* [♣] the *Ace of Spades* and returns a small trump.

West is in, North's trump problems are solved and what's next? West could attack diamonds, but continues spades and North trumps the fourth round. North plays *Ace then Queen of Hearts*. East covers with the *Heart King* around to West's *Ace,* who then leads another spade. North ruffs with the *Ten of Clubs*, East helplessly under-ruffing with his smaller trump. North plays another heart, to East's *Ace.*

East would do better playing a trump [♣], but instead leads the fourth *Ace of Hearts*, and plays hearts until South finally ruffs. South then leads the *Queen of Diamonds* to North's *Ace* who then returns the *Jack of Diamonds* to put East on the spot.

If East rises with the *Ace of Diamonds* he gets only 2 counters, if he plays the *King*, South sticks in the *Ten*. East postpones the decision by playing the *Ace of Diamonds* on the diamond lead and pushing back the sixth heart for North to trump. That gives East/West 16 HCP.

This is the position after 16 tricks when North now plays the *King of Diamonds*:

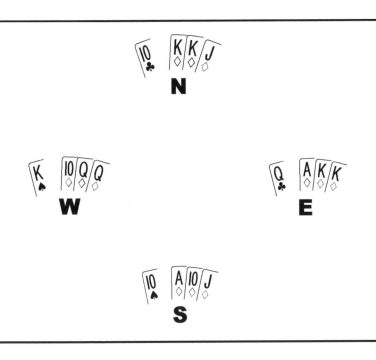

The *King of Diamonds* forces East's *Ace*, allowing South to take the last three tricks. The *Ten of Spades* is trumped by North's *Ten of Clubs* and South's *Ace* and *Ten of Diamonds* clean things up for 31 HCP.

Was there a possibility of a save for East/West? What if East had played a trump at each opportunity? That would have prevented South from ruffing the fifth heart.

You usually want to force the Declarer to ruff so that he loses trump control, but you hardly ever want his partner to get in the act and start trumping for him.

That's why the defenders often need to lead trump also, even when Declarer chooses not to do so. Let me amend that, *especially* when Declarer chooses not to do so. Because, what's bad for the bidder has to be good for the defenders.

This is probably the hardest thing to teach new players, <u>when</u> to lead trumps!

"He Passed a <u>59</u> Bid!"

*If you cannot recall why everyone is so incredulous at this pass, go back to page 75 and read again the section under the heading **How High Should I Jump Bid?** and you will be sure not to make the same mistake as this player.*

Giving It All Away

The next hand demonstrates a problem resulting from not sending the meld promptly. This East/West couple actually had the hand stolen from them. (Or did they give it away?)

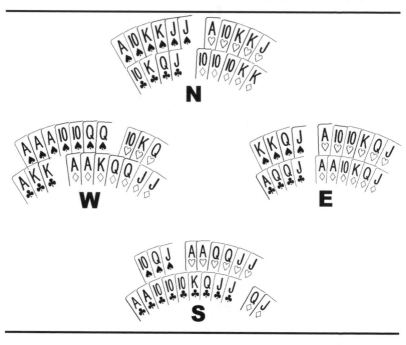

EAST	SOUTH	WEST	NORTH
50	65	Pass	Pass
Pass	Clubs		

Although East had considerable power, he never let his partner know what he had. West could only assume there was not enough meld to take the bid. Thus the opposition had no competition. Confessionals are generally confidential, but the following was overheard as South recounted today's hand:

"Father, I have sinned."

"What was your sin my child?"

"A sin of commission, last night I stole this bid from the opponents. When the meld came down East was saying; 'Partner, I wish I knew you had that much meld, we could have made a hundred!' *That's when I knew I had stolen the hand."*

"What did you do then?"

"I opened up with my double ace of hearts and then tried to see what I could catch in clubs. Nothing big fell, so I continued the hearts. My partner got in and picked up my ten of spades then he played hearts again. That's when West's ace of clubs showed up. He played three more rounds of spades so I cut the third one and played another heart. Now East was in and started the diamonds. I cut the third one and played another heart. My partner cut in since he still had a trump and then played another spade. East cut with the queen but I over-cut and then gave him his ace of clubs for their last trick. I couldn't sleep at all after this, so what will be my penance?"

"My child, an Honest Confession is Good for the Soul. But no penance is necessary in this case since you committed no sin. West was at fault for not sending meld to his partner. Your bid of 65 was merely a nuisance. Nothing prevented him from jumping the bidding by 10 or 15 to show either 30 or 40 meld. Especially since he held 6 aces with a partner who had already opened the bidding. East too was in full complicity, since he also could have opened the bidding with a jump to show his meld. I can plainly see that no theft was involved here. They gave this hand to you willingly!'

"Thank you Father."

CHAPTER 6 - OPENER'S REBIDS
"I like quiet opponents.
Usually it means they're not getting good hands."

Once Responder has sent the meld, it is now usually up to the Opener to place the contract. Often a direct jump to the highest level one expects to make will suffice. At other times Opener may bid up gradually to get the bid as cheap as possible. In any case, you want to make sure that the opposition does not steal your '**spot**'.

What is your spot? That is the bidding level beyond which you cannot pass without getting set. For example, if your hand plus your partners meld will allow you to make a maximum of 65, that is your '**spot**'.

Suppose on this hand rather than bidding 65, your spot, you bid instead another lower number and the opponents bid 65. They have stolen your spot! If you now bid 70, you are in danger of going down. Check out the next set.

Pick Your Spot, Then Go to It

South's jump to 60 crowded the bidding but was not well thought out. What did South intend to do if West bid 65? Could he then go to 70? His 19 points plus partner's 20, would require 31 in HCP. Does he have a hand that is likely to pull 31 High Card Points?

The answers to these questions should dictate the more prudent bid of 65, rather than 60. If West chooses to go to 70, Let Him!

Review the example below:

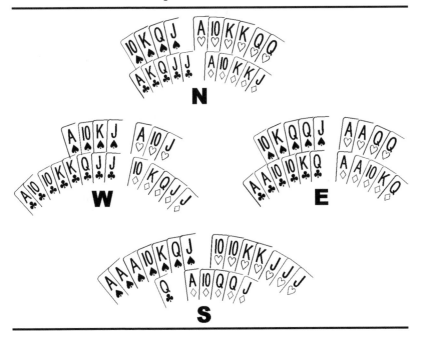

NORTH	EAST	SOUTH	WEST
52	54	60	65
Pass	Pass	70 {??}	Pass
		Spades	

As it stands, the only chance for success, would be for South to make the unlikely opening of a diamond. North would then be able to cash the heart and club aces, preventing the save and making the bid in the process.

Unfortunately, South driving a factory equipped model without the extra chrome, wire wheels and X-ray vision, was unable to see this opening and led the *Queen of Spades* instead. West immediately rose with the *Ace of Spades*, then cashed the *Ace of Hearts* and *Ace of Clubs*. The club exit started South ruffing right away.

South now led the *King of Hearts* to North's *Ace* and hearts were continued. East won and forced South with another club. South's heart return was ruffed by West catching East's *Ace*.

West's club return forced South to ruff this time with the *Spade Ten*. Now South started the diamonds to clear up the end game leading the *Queen of Diamonds*. West made the Key play of the *Ten* here, which forced out North's *Ace*.

North then played the *Ten* to force out one of East's *Ace* stoppers in the *Diamond* suit.

Here East made the best play of a small spade, taking South's *Ace* out of play.

South's *Queen of Diamonds* now brought North's *Ten* and East's last stopper in Diamonds, the *Ace*.

East's fifth club makes South trump with an *Ace of Spades*. South gets out with the *King of Hearts* trumped by West's *Ten of Spades*.

The sixth club denudes South of the last *Ace of Spades*, and the *Ten of Hearts* is led, hoping to clear the trump suit. West pitches the *Ten of Clubs* as East trumps with the *Queen of Spades* and cashes the *Ten of Spades* for 24 HCP.

The last two tricks go to North/South with *Ace* and *Ten of Diamonds*.

That's a lot of sweat to get only 26 points and go set. Why not just bid what you can make, 65?

Bid with Your Head, Not Your Ego

Often, one must forego the natural human tendencies of jealousy, rage, revenge and spite to be successful at Pinochle. All Pinochle aficionados have their favorite story of emotions that ran wild.

This tale concerns one player, a Mr. Franklin, charged with manslaughter after an argument over a Pinochle bid. There were two players that had little respect for each other's game, Mr. Franklin and the dearly departed. These two were forced into a partnership this particular night, because another player had failed to show up and the host's wife was roped into the game as a substitute. She would <u>only</u> play with her husband.

As the night wore down, so did the game and temper of the two protagonists. The crowning moment occurred when the deceased opened the bidding at 50 and Mr. Franklin bid 59. He was left in this bid with double aces and without a marriage when his partner passed (with a run). The deceased gave as an excuse for his action the fact that Franklin had previously passed him out after a 30 meld bid (probably a double pinochle).

Needless to say, tempers flared, the argument escalated, the two were asked to leave and the final hand was played out on the street, with no eye witnesses.

Mr. Franklin secured for his defense a famous attorney who was also an avid Pinochle enthusiast, and could thus empathize with his plight.

The day of the trial found Mr. Franklin at the defense table with a Pinochle deck, his barrister and two other players to assist in the defense.

After packing the jury with as many Pinochle players as he could find, the lawyer then returned to the defense table and started a game by beginning to deal the cards. Of course the judge interrupted the proceedings and demanded that the cards be put away, and that the fourth player, (who had his back to the judge's bench) return to the other side of the table.

The attorney asked to approach the bench and explained that the game was necessary and appropriate for the proper defense of his client's case, as the flavor and setting of the fatal night would thus be re-enacted and aid his case.

After much deliberation and objections by the prosecution, the judge ruled that the game could continue within certain limits. No oral bids would be permitted, they must either sign with their fingers or write the bids down, and there would be no shuffling of the cards, in order to preserve the dignity of the court.

You can imagine what a spectacle was presented to the jury as the trial proceeded with the four people at the defense table making signs and slapping cards, oblivious to the expert witnesses and officials on the stand. Add to this, the sight of a butler in full uniform coming in and out of the courtroom with pre-shuffled cards on a silver serving platter.

Consequently it was hardly a surprise to courtroom buffs when the jury after only ten minutes deliberation, brought back a verdict of not guilty due to temporary insanity.

The judge however, not as easily impressed, determined that the temporary nature of the insanity was questionable. Therefore, Mr. Franklin was remanded to the custody of the Superintendent of the State Institution for the Criminally Insane, to be kept under close observation for an indefinite period.

CHAPTER 7 - COMPETITIVE BIDDING
"Remember that you're not 'all that',
there are 3 other people involved here".

When both teams are in the auction bidding fast and furious, fortune often favors the bold. If you are inclined to be conservative in your bidding approach, you may be pre-empted out of many hands that should be yours. Besides, remember the adage, *"If you never get set, then you're not bidding enough."*

Note what happens in the following hand when East does not take the bull by the horns and bid his full potential. As it stands either East or South can probably pull 60-65 points in their respective suits because the power is equally distributed.

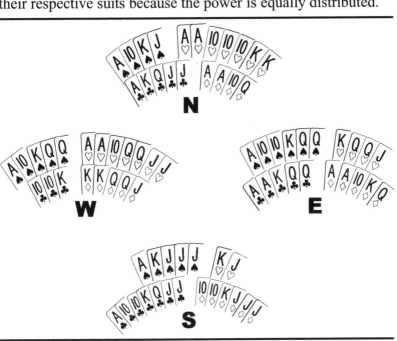

SOUTH	WEST	NORTH	EAST
50	Pass	51	52
53	Pass	Pass	60
65			Pass
Clubs			

South had the advantage of bidding first, and chose to open this weak hand with the minimum-opening bid of 50. North made the key bid of 51, which worked out well.

Many recommend a one-over bid to show 12-16 meld, because 10 points is expected even when partner has not bid. Using the **SCAMP** Bidding System, we would have elected to send 52 as meld, counting our extra aces.

In this case, North reasoned that 12 points coupled with six aces made a sound case for the simple overcall of 51. East now had an opportunity to take advantage of this lapse and shine for his side. Playing his partner for the expected average of 10 points, and holding 24 meld of his own, he could have reasonable expectations of making 60.

Had East bid 60 bid at this point, the bidding space would have been effectively choked up, giving South a dilemma with such a weak hand. Instead East chose to woodenly bid 52, giving South a chance to get more information.

When South carried on to 53 and North passed, South understood that North's 51 bid was based on a hand good for a single bid, but not quite strong enough for a jump bid. South then had no problem in persisting to 65 over East's belated 60.

Had North bid a second time, it would have shown a strongly distributional hand, which might play best in North's suit. As it turns out South makes 65 handily but is unable to stop the save by East/West.

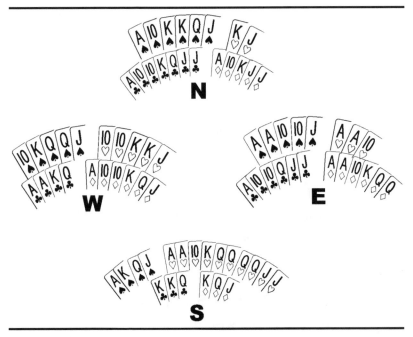

Got a Hunch? Bid a Bunch!

Got a hunch? Bid a bunch! is the theme of this hand. South has no reservations in stretching the bidding to 85. With 39 points in hand and a 20 jump from partner, note that South does not simply bid 80 in hopes that West will pass.

South accurately reasons that 85 is the top of their range, and therefore jumps to 85 rather than allow West to possibly bid it first and steal their spot.

Watch how South jumps to the final bid on the hand as shown, in the table presented below:

WEST	NORTH	EAST	SOUTH
52	54	56	60
65	Pass	Pass	70
75			85
Pass			Hearts

Listening to the bidding, you should deduce that East who only shows 12 meld, must have at least six to seven aces to justify her 20 meld bid. That's why good players not only follow the bidding, but also watch the melds carefully. It helps one decide which card is best for a lead[20]. There's always more to your opponent's hand than what the meld shows you.

South wants to reach partner quickly, hoping partner can pick up South's losers in the short suits. Even if West gets in first, he must still negotiate a safe passage through the North hand if East/West expect to save their meld.

South does well by finding the optimum lead of the *Ace of Spades*, continuing with the *King of Spades* to reach partner. North promptly cashes the diamond and club aces, effectively slamming the door on the East/West meld.

After all, there's very little percentage in making 87 on a hand, if you still allow the opponents to save 55. Much better, you make 92 and they save only the memories.

Don't Make Your Partner Bid Blind

All too many otherwise decent players neglect to send meld when they have a run in their own hand. In this hand South had an anemic trump suit and support for all suits. So with seven aces and 16 meld, South opted to give a 20-meld bid instead. Now partner was allowed to make the final call.

---

[20]This topic will be discussed more thoroughly in the next chapter.

On the West side of town nothing of value was shown. Then East compounded the problem by keeping West in the dark. So, even with a possible 60-65 point hand between them, it's simply criminal to see this team come up empty.

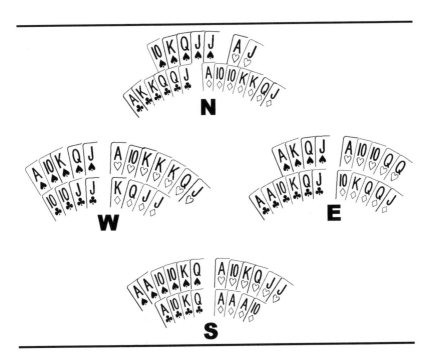

SOUTH	WEST	NORTH	EAST
52	53	54	55
56	57	58	Pass
Pass	60	70	
	Pass	Diamonds	

Using RAM's **SCAMP** Bidding System, South's hand would qualify for a 30-meld jump bid. (With 16 Meld, plus 1 point each for the first four aces and 3 points for each ace over four, the hand counts up to 29.)

South using conventional bidding can only bid 52. West shows a suit at 53 and North simply bids one over. East did not feel strong enough for a jump, but was reluctant to pass with 16 points and four aces.

South's bid of 56 was a check-back indicating a suit and asking if North really wants the bid. North accepts the gauntlet with a 70 bid which pre-empts the opponents.

In case West decides 70 is a good spot, North wants to be there first. You feel so stupid when you nickel and dime the bidding and the opponents take the highest bid you had a chance to make.

Play of the hand was unspectacular; East/West had no chance to save. Actually, the most they can make is five tricks, maybe only four if they're not careful. Had West taken the bid in hearts however, this story would have a different ending.

Moral: Always Send the Meld First, you can usually bid again later if your hand is that strong. If you don't send the meld, the hand could be taken away and neither you nor your partner may get the bid.

What's a [Good] Barricade Bid?

A warning here about the habit of some players to bid 60 as a barricade bid to inhibit the opponents from winning the bid. It is largely ineffective in today's modern bidding. An exercise in the numbers will show why this is so.

Say your LHO opens the bidding at 50, and your partner passes. Your RHO now bids 52 showing 20 meld, and you jump to 60. Your 60 may be based on a hand like this:

In short, you are hoping that your partner will contribute 10 points to the war effort, which will put you over with 60 points, if and when you can pull 21 HCP.

What is your LHO thinking? Maybe with a hand like this one below:

With 21 meld in hand, and partner sending 20, all they need is a save to make 60. It is therefore no big deal to bid 65, which is only five more.

What would LHO be thinking however, if you bid 65? Now they must weigh the possibilities of going in the hole for 70. Maybe they will bid it, and go in the hole.

The least you can do, is to give them a chance to try it. Bidding 60 is like saying OK, go ahead and take it.

So what if they pass your 65 bid and you miss it? As long as you don't let them save, what harm could it do? They were going to make 60 or 65 anyway, now you are in the hole for 65. What's the difference? Their plus 65 is the same score as minus 65 for you.

Here is another hand that demonstrates the point. South reasonably has a play for 65 if partner has the expected 10 points. Had South bid only 60, East/West may very well take a chance at 65:

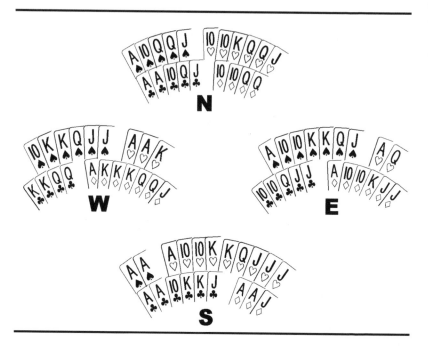

NORTH	EAST	SOUTH	WEST
Pass	50	65	Pass
	Pass	Wins Bid	

You can readily see that 65 is a highly attainable range when partner responds with a 20 jump after you open the bidding. You can more effectively use the 60 bid, at times when you are trying to push the opponents to 65.

PART 3 - PLAY OF THE HAND

CHAPTER 8 - OPENING LEADS
"I start every hand with a plan. So does my partner.
Unfortunately, they are seldom the same."

Selecting the proper opening lead can be crucial to the success or failure of a bid. Usually one is guided by features such as (*Shape)* of the hand, amount of power (*Aces,*) bidding sequence, meld shown, time of month, phase of the moon, disposition of partner, and so on.

Examples in this chapter will show how distribution or *Shape* of the hand influences ones lead. Say you are stuck with fairly even distribution, 6-5-5-4, 6-6-4-4, 7-5-4-4, or even the ghastly 5-5-5-5 hand! With no other information available, you should normally attempt to get the opponent's top trumps off your back.

Hopefully, this will allow you to score that all-important last trick bonus. Although many neophytes put off this task until last, sooner or later like a bad tooth, it has to come out.

Often the very act of pushing trump allows one to reach partner who may have information to share, aiding you in directing the play.

Tipping off Your Partner
In any event, your opening lead will alert partner to your concerns. For example, playing your outside aces first indicates that you may be short-suited and don't want your aces trapped.

Play of one or more aces in a particular suit coupled with a continuation, indicates length in that suit and a desire to make someone trump it. Possibly their trump holding will be weakened or Opener's trumps promoted.

When the bidder's partner has melded aces, it is almost self evident that a trump lead is called for. An exception to this rule is usually when the bidder is short in a suit. Then the bidder will usually play any aces from that suit first to avoid them being trapped.

Learning How to Pick Your Lead Cards

In the following examples, with no guidance from the bidding or meld, what lead would you use to open the hand?

Sample Hand 8a:

K Q J ♠♠♠   A 10 10 K K Q J ♡♡♡♡♡♡♡   10 Q J ♣♣♣   A A 10 K K Q J ♢♢♢♢♢♢♢

Make hearts trump, start with double *Ace of Diamonds* and continue the suit at every opportunity to induce ruffing by your partner, the opponents or both. Hopefully the opponents will be forced to cut and weaken their trump holding.

Sample Hand 8b:

10 K K Q Q J J ♠♠♠♠♠♠♠   A A Q ♡♡♡   A A 10 10 K K Q J J ♣♣♣♣♣♣♣♣♣   Q ♢

With clubs trump, we would again start the long side suit to force opponents trumps out. We probably will be forced to ruff in diamonds right away. We are not too keen about cashing out our heart aces right away as we view it more important to get the spade suit in play. [Hopefully partner will avoid playing side suit aces that allow our aces to be trapped.]

Sample Hand 8c:

| A A 10 K Q Q J ♠ | A Q J J J ♡ | A K Q Q ♣ | A 10 K Q ♢ |

With spades as trump, our partner's meld indicates holding a few aces. Open right away with *Queen of Spades*. Partner will recognize that our failure to cash any aces means we want the trump out. If the trump lead goes all the way around to RHO, we will then cash our aces at first opportunity and still push the trump suit.

If you conclude that partner is short aces on this hand, there is no need to preserve your outside aces. Cash them out first and push the heart suit in hopes that partner can cut the fourth or fifth one.

Sample Hand 8d:

| A A A 10 10 Q Q J ♠ | K K Q Q ♡ | Q Q ♣ | A A 10 K Q Q ♢ |

Having made diamonds trump here, a save is our prime consideration. Spades are semi-solid, however, our trumps are decent but scanty. We are aware that we may be forced (to trump) clubs. If this happens early, we could lose control of the hand very quickly. To prepare for this possibility, we elect to go on the offensive by playing the spades. With only six trumps, we prefer to get the opponents trumping before us.

The 12 outstanding spades are probably divided 5-4-3, 6-4-2 or 6-3-3, with the *Ace* likely to be in the hand with the 5 or 6. We don't care if we catch the *Ace* or pick up the suit. We simply wish to get the opponents ruffing before they force us to trump. On this hand timing is paramount, so we start out with triple *Ace of Spades* confident that the third or fourth round will be trumped. After that we will continue to play the spade suit every chance we get. Hopefully the hand holding the most of our trumps, will also be the one trumping the spades.

Sample Hand 8e:

A K J J J ♠ A A A 10 K Q J J ♥ 10 K K Q Q J ♣ K ♦

On this hand your trumps [♥] have the same odds as your spade holding on the last hand. The singleton in your hand raises the possibility of a singleton in another hand.

So cash the *Ace of Spades* first, then push the club suit until someone ruffs in.

Sample Hand 8f:

A A Q Q J ♠ A 10 K K ♥ A 10 10 10 K K K Q J ♣ J J ♦

Your nine trumps [♣] are not yet established, so try to promote your trump holding by trump leads. The odds favor them being divided 4-4-3 or 5-4-2 but in this case the simple play of the *Queen of Clubs* removes at least one of the top three honors. Hold your stoppers in the side suits for now, since playing the side aces reveals your weakness in diamonds.

Sample Hand 8g:

10 K Q Q ♠ A 10 K Q Q Q J ♥ A A Q Q J ♣ A 10 10 J ♦

You can do nothing with this hand unless your partner has a fit with your trumps and some trick taking potential. You may as well assume this is true. In that case partner will need the trumps [♥] removed. Bite the bullet early and open with the *Queen of Trumps.*

Sample Hand 8h:

| A 10 J J J | A 10 J J J J | Q J | A 10 K K K Q Q J |
| ♠ ♠ ♠ ♠ ♠ | ♡ ♡ ♡ ♡ ♡ | ♣ ♣ | ◇ ◇ ◇ ◇ ◇ ◇ ◇ ◇ |

This is a tough one. You have two choices, one, is to try to reach partner with trump [♦] and hope that he will pick off a couple of your losers.

Another option, pick one of the side suits, play your ace and continue it in hopes of reaching him that way. Don't play both side suit aces; hopefully you may get to promote one of your tens into a trick after a lead by your LHO.

Sample Hand 8i:

| A 10 K K Q J | J | 10 Q Q Q J | 10 K K K Q Q J J |
| ♠ ♠ ♠ ♠ ♠ ♠ | ♡ | ♣ ♣ ♣ ♣ ♣ | ◇ ◇ ◇ ◇ ◇ ◇ ◇ ◇ |

We assume you made spades trumps for points (from the run), but we wouldn't have faulted you for naming diamonds.

Both suits are anemic and we imagine this hand was dropped on you as the dealer.

Anyway, open with the *Queen of Diamonds* and keep pushing diamonds every time you get the lead. If forced to use trump, ruff with a counter at every opportunity.

Making this 20 HCP will be like pulling teeth. Basically, you want to hurry up and get on with the next hand.

Sample Hand 8j:

On many hands observing the meld may suggest an opening lead you'd otherwise overlook. On this hand the bid is dropped on you. You call clubs trumps. (Remember that you have to name trump before you get to see your partner's meld.)

The meld is displayed as follows:

K♠ Q♠ J♦

(North)

J♠ K♡ K♡ Q♡ Q♡ J♡ K♦ Q♦ J♦ J♣ (West)

A♠ K♠ K♠ Q♠ Q♠ A♡ A♣ A♦ K♦ Q♦ (East)

This is your hand (as South):

10♠ Q♠ J♠ A♡ A♡ 10♡ K♡ Q♡ A♣ K♣ K♣ Q♣ Q♣ J♣ J♣ A♦ 10♦ Q♦ J♦ J♦

You want to reach partner before the RHO gets the lead. The five hearts West shows and the bare ace by East, suggest RHO may be short in hearts.

You lead double *Ace of Hearts* and partner follows with the *Ten* and *Queen*. Your *King of Hearts* to partner's *Ace* catches RHO's *Ace*. Partner continues with *Ace of Spades* and double *Ace of Diamonds*. (Expert tip: Give partner your *Queen* on the first *Ace of Diamonds*, and the *Jack* on the next one.) This gives you the potential for two more tricks in *Diamonds* after West's *Ace* is gone. Partner should not continue the *Diamonds,* instead partner should continue *Hearts* to get West cutting, and use up his trump.

Always watch the meld (comparing what you see with the bidding). It doesn't hurt if you can remember it for a second or two after everyone picks the cards up, too.

Playing to Get Opponents HCP

Here is a hand I witnessed a friend play in South Carolina, USA that was subsequently published in my Pinochle Passion column. It demonstrates how to count your tricks and find ways to cash them out. Also, it tells how to gauge your limit and bid it before the opponents do.

Fannie, playing South, could certainly count her points. With her 35 plus 10 points from partner, it would leave her needing 25 in HCP.

East counting up his 27 points and adding partners 20, should have seen that 70 was the spot for him. Instead, he played the waiting game and allowed Fannie to bid it first.

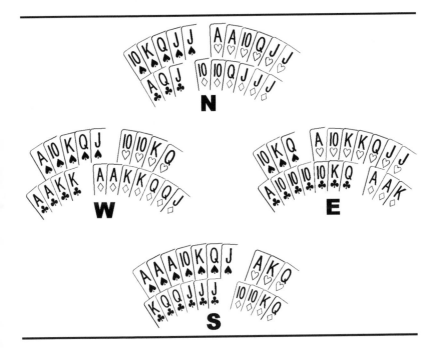

See below how East lets Fannie hit her spot first?

WEST	NORTH	EAST	SOUTH
52	Pass	60	70
Pass		Pass	Spades

With a run melded on the left, 23 HCP would be no walk in the park. Fannie, always resourceful, saw the chance to slip one over on West. So, after cashing the *Ace of Hearts*, Fannie casually flipped out the *Jack of Trump* [♠].

West covered with the *Queen of Trump* [♠], preserving a point and hoping to retain his *Ace* and *Ten of Spades*, for two trump tricks. North stepped up with the *Ten*, cashed his *Aces* and returned a club.

East won the *Ace* and blithely ignored the danger of North trumping his good clubs. Instead of pushing trump[♠], he cashed two *Aces of Diamonds* and the *Ace of Hearts*. Fannie trumped in with the *King of Spades*, and led the third *Club*.

Too late, West saw the plan and belatedly led trump [♠] but Fannie won and pushed another club for North to munch on. The heart return was trumped high by Fannie and another *Club* was cut, this time by West with the *Ten*, who then played his *Ace of Spades* and two *Diamond Aces*.

Fannie still had a club to lose but was content with 28 for a fine score. Good defense would have held her to 20, for minus 70. Sadly enough, on hands like these one or both of the defenders often walk away unaware that their slips are showing.

Play Your Partner's Cards Too

I played this hand in Fairbanks Alaska using partner's *Ten*, without his knowledge. I had the South cards:

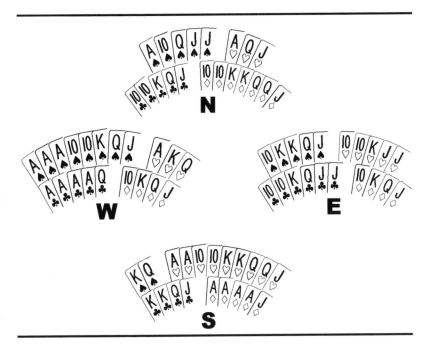

WEST	NORTH	EAST	SOUTH
50	52	53	60
65	Pass	Pass	70
80			85
Pass			Hearts

North started this free-for-all with his minimal 20-meld bid. Then East had the nerve to enter the bidding with a horrible hand, but still 22 points. That was all the excuse West needed to push the bid into the rarified air of the 80's.

I would not be denied and persisted to 85 hoping for a little bit more from my partner. When the meld came down, I found myself needing 36, and had to solve a timeless problem. How to get to my partner, without getting slapped up side the head on the way over.

West, on the bidding, was almost certainly marked with *Aces* in every suit except *Diamonds*. West's marriage in trumps [♥] precluded my picking off that *Ace*. I devised what could be an elegant solution, provided West would cooperate.

First I played the *Ace of Trumps* [♥], North showing the *Queen*. Then I led the *Jack of Diamonds* covered by the *Queen of Diamonds*.

My partner, North, was more than pleasantly surprised to see his *Ten* stand up, shall we say flabbergasted? Glad for this opportunity, he took the *Ace of Spades* and after a slight hesitation, the *Ace of Hearts*.

My play of the first *Ace of Hearts* was in hopes of inducing North to play his *Ace* if he had it, rather than waiting for a push. After cashing out and with nothing else to say, North passed the baton back to me via the trump suit [♥].

Even before my *Ace of Hearts* came up, West started shaking his head. He realized the missed opportunity of rising with the *Ten of Diamonds*.

East/West still pulled a spade and four club tricks, but our 37 points were already a matter of record for a nice score of 86 points total.

Try to Have Fun

A hand that I'm not so proud of occurred in Oakland CA when I was visiting there.

My cousin Anita took me by the home of some locally famous players. They were looking to take my measure and I was anxious to get started with a bang.

I got my chance on the first hand, when the RHO said regarding me: *"Man he looks serious, I better not fool around here, I bid 90."*

Right away I said to the LHO: *"I pass, 90 on you!,"*

He said: *"My partner was just fooling around, he doesn't really bid 90."* I was not amenable to let him change and held him to the bid. They started off 90 in the hole, but the whole complexion of the evening changed.

I have since learned to be more flexible and take care to do nothing that's going to take away from other's enjoyment of the game.

If someone wants to fool around a little, let them enjoy themselves, since the whole purpose of the game should be wholesome entertainment.

[If we're out for blood, maybe some of our own will get spilled along the way.]

CHAPTER 9 - MANAGING YOUR TRUMP

"Learn to cut your partner some slack, but if he fashions a noose, don't stick your neck in it!"

Declarer, after viewing the meld and having the most knowledge of the trump situation must make the first call on how the trumps should be handled. This call, is of course subject to modification by partner, and most assuredly by the defenders, who certainly are under no obligation to accept Declarer's assessment of trump play.

However, on the first trick anyway, the ball is in the Declarer's court. Declarer's first responsibility, is to set the tone for the contract by the first play.

Will Declarer postpone trump handling until more important matters are taken care of, or set out immediately to remove those *'thorns in the flesh '* ?

In the next example, first we present the bidding:

NORTH	EAST	SOUTH	WEST
			Pass
50	Pass	51	
Pass		Clubs	

As you will see, North made a minimal opening bid to avoid dropping the bid on his partner, the dealer. South's bid takes North off the hook in case North's hand is minimal. North is willing to pass with support for all suits.

Start with Trump or Off Suit?

Here are all of the full hands:

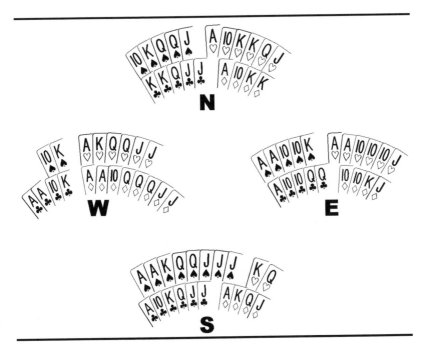

South's view of the meld and her unbalanced hand, (6-8-4-2) make her avoid leading trump [♣], and try instead, to run the opponents out of trump. If that fails, South may find that her partner is able to trump the losing spades if trump is not drawn.

South's six lonely trump might soon get swallowed up if the opponents find a heart lead early enough. Accordingly South opens a spade and continues them at every opportunity.

Follow along with the play of the entire hand and see how minimal trump can be used to advantage, even with a short off-suit (non trump suit.)

#	North	East	South	West
1	10♠	K♠	▶A♠	K♠
2	K♠	10♠	▶A♠	10♠
3	J♠	10♠	▶Q♠	K♣
4	J♥	10♥	Q♥	▶A♥
5	A♥	J♥	K♥	▶J♥
6	▶Q♠	A♠	J♠	10♣
North. Continues the pressure with the spades.				
7	J♣	10♣	J♣	▶A♣
8	J♣	Q♣	J♣	▶A♣
9	K♥	10♥	K♣	▶J♥
10	Q♠	A♠	▶J♠	K♥
11	K♥	▶10♥	10♣	Q♥
12	Q♣	10♣	▶J♠	10♦
13	K♣	▶A♣	Q♣	J♦
14	10♥	▶A♥	A♣	Q♥
15	K♣	Q♣	▶Q♠	J♦
16	▶K♦	10♦	A♦	Q♦
17	Q♥	J♦	▶K♠	Q♦
The spade finally walks alone.				
18	K♦	K♦	▶Q♦	A♦
19	10♦	10♦	J♦	▶A♦
20	A♦	A♥	K♦	▶Q♦
North/South makes 29 HCP.				

So we see that even a shortage of trump will not kill us if we use our long suit (spades in this case) to our advantage.

Low Trumps Still Beat Aces

No matter how well you play, sooner or later you'll run into the Master Meld Holder and his partner, who pulls his fat out of the fire just when you have him burning best!

Notice the following example:

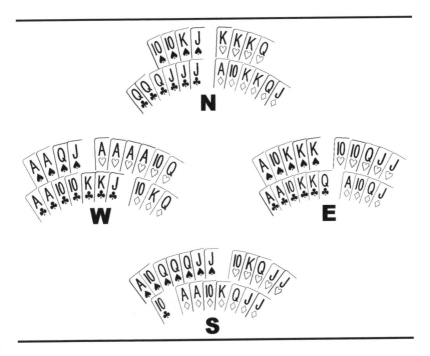

SOUTH	WEST	NORTH	EAST
60	Pass	Pass	Pass
Diamonds			

Today's Declarer was one of those characters you always meet on the <u>opposite</u> side of the table. Never on <u>your</u> side. Partner ever ready to rescue him.

I learned early in my career never to expect this kind of support when I am in this position. The opponents it seems, always do. How can you bid, counting on your partner to have a run with you? UnReal!

South went after trumps with the *Queen of Diamonds*, reaching partner. What little hope South had was dashed when partner was unable to play one *Ace* before returning trump.

I held the West cards on this deal. I was smiling inwardly at the surprise South was about to get as he went down.

#	North	East	South	West
1	A♦	J♦	►Q♦	K♦
2	►Q♦	A♦	J♦	10♦
3	J♣	►A♣	10♣	K♣
4	J♣	►A♣	K♦	J♣
5	Q♥	10♥	►Q♥	10♥
6	J♣	Q♣	J♦	►10♣
I figured, why not keep him cutting.				
7	K♥	10♥	►J♥	A♥
8	Q♣	K♣	10♦	►A♣
9	K♥	J♥	►J♥	A♥
10	Q♣	10♣	A♦	►K♣
11	K♥	J♥	►K♥	A♥
12	K♦	10♦	A♦	►Q♦
That must be his last trump.				
13	J♦	Q♥	►10♥	A♥
His partner comes to his rescue, what now?				

This is the position after Trick 13.

N

W

E

S

Now let's follow the play of the rest of the hand:

#	North	East	South	West
14	▶10♠	A♠	J♠	J♠
North. Inspired lead {!!} knocks out my Partner's (East) spade stopper.				
15	Q♣	▶K♣	J♠	A♣
East. Trump would be no better.				
16	K♦	Q♦	Q♠	▶10♣
17	▶K♠	10♠	A♠	Q♠
Saving their meld at this point!				
18	J♠	K♠	▶Q♠	A♠
19	10♦	K♠	10♠	▶Q♥
20	▶10♠	K♠	Q♠	A♠

I couldn't believe they made 24 HCP on this hand with only four aces. There's no justice for just us.

"The Official Ruling"

"I'm afraid that it is <u>her</u> trick Sir."... "But she trumped it with the <u>Ace</u>, Sir." ... "No Sir, you can't overtrump her ace, she played it <u>first</u>!." ... "Sorry Sir, you can't take <u>back</u> your ace, either."

Living with the 'Must Trump' Rule

Trump management can be a pain sometimes with the Must Trump rule. When Declarer's trumps are short, defenders can force him to ruff, using up his trumps and losing control of the hand. His trumps may quickly evaporate into thin air.

Here trump management skills come dear. On such hands, knowing he may be forced to ruff prematurely, Declarer may choose to defer drawing trumps. Instead, he may introduce his own long suit first, hoping to induce ruffing by the defenders, as illustrated in the hand below that was taken from a Duplicate Pinochle game, where several players play the same hands for comparison.

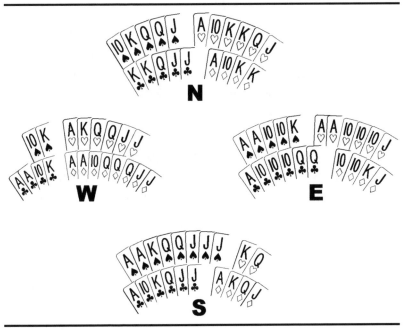

WEST	NORTH	EAST	SOUTH
Pass	50	Pass	51
	Pass		Clubs

Because South's trump holding was scanty, he was moved to look for a method of pulling trump less hazardous to the health of his hand. Fortunately he possessed such a tool in his eight-card side suit, spades. Leading out with double *Ace of Spades* and another spade produced the desired result, as West found his trumps under attack. He attempted to counter with an attack on diamonds, playing double *Ace of Diamonds* and the *Queen*. North was now in with the *Ace of Diamonds* and saw no reason to change partner's tactics. So after cashing the *Ace of Hearts*, he brought another spade to bear on West.

West now reduced to double *Ace of Clubs*, decided not to use them on ruffs, and accordingly cashed them out. Persisting with diamonds he pushed the fourth round ending in the South hand. South offered up another small spade, the fifth, won by East. Double *Ace of Hearts* was led and the second trumped by South with the *King of Clubs*. Back again came the ubiquitous spade. North trumps with the *Queen of Clubs*, overtaken by East's *Ten*.

South trumps the fourth heart (with the *Ten* this time.) *Ace of Clubs* is cashed picking up the *King* from North and *Ten* from East. Then the seventh spade finishes off East who must trump with the *Ace of Clubs*. South's last two tricks are the *Queen of Trumps* [♣] and the eighth spade. Makes 32 HCP.

How does this hand stack up using **SCAMP**'s hand evaluation? With this holding South can add 9 points for **Shape** on this hand due to the long side suit, 20 for **Count**, 4 for **Aces** and 39 for **Meld**. Add 11 for **Partner** [deducts 5 points for having only two aces]. By using **SCAMP**'s evaluation, we total up 82 points. Actual points made: 87.

My wife says; once I get involved in a Pinochle game, nothing else matters. I disagree. When I play, everything else matters. I just don't allow it to distract me. Some folks call Pinochle players extremists, I think they're harmless, as they tend to get in a corner all by themselves and bother no one.

I heard of one such player who regularly drove a Yugo. He happened to pull up at a traffic signal where a Rolls Royce was waiting. Since the window was down he shouted over, *"Say, you got a phone in there?"*

Naturally the reply came, '***Yes, I have a telephone.***'

Back went, *"I got a phone in my Yugo too!"*
    '***Okay.***'

Next the inquiry, *"Say, you got a TV?"*
    '***Yes, my Rolls has a television.***'

"I got a TV in my Yugo too."
    '***Well, OK.***'

"How about a GPS, you got a GPS?"
    Again the assurance that it was standard equipment on a Rolls.

"What about a card table?"
    Yes the Rolls had a card table.

"How about a BED, do you have a bed? My Yugo has a bed."

At this the Rolls owner peeled rubber, ashamed to admit that his car had no bed.

Next stop, the Rolls Royce Dealer. '*I want a bed installed in my Rolls, Right Now!*' Nothing would mollify the owner until assured that the bed would be ordered and airlifted that night, installed the next day, cost being no object. Early morning found the owner at the dealer waiting, he actually hung around all day until the bed was installed, complete with brass headboard, chrome springs and silk sheets.

Delivery was made at 4pm. Next, the ride around town all evening, looking for the Yugo. Finally, the Yugo is spotted parked on a side street.

The Rolls blew the horn with no response. It was obvious that the Yugo was occupied as all the windows were fogged up.

A rap on the window which produced a response from within. Three men sitting at a Pinochle table were asked for the owner of the Yugo. They said he was busy but would be out soon as they were waiting for him to start the game. This brought an insistence that he be found at once. Mr. Yugo soon appeared with a towel around his neck and was asked:

'*Do you remember me?*' queried the Rolls owner.

"*Yes, aren't you the guy driving the Rolls Royce that I talked to yesterday?*"

'*That's right, and I want you to know that I now have a bed installed in my Rolls.*'

Mr. Yugo replied sadly, shaking his head: "*I can't Believe, that you got me out of the shower, just to tell me That!*"

When Should You be a Sandbagger?

On this next hand, I'd prefer if you don't ask how South made it all the way up to 70 holding only two aces, OK?

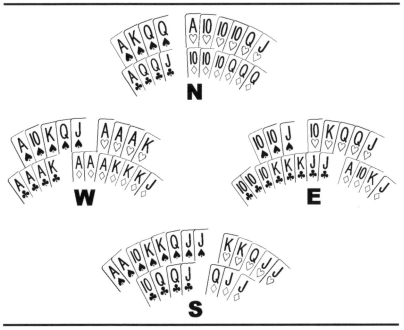

EAST	SOUTH	WEST	NORTH
Pass	50	51	57
	60	65	Pass
	70	Pass	
	Spades		

South now needs 31 HCPs and tries the *Spade Queen* on for size. *"Don't worry partner,"* West assured, *"I'm not a Sandbagger!"* With that, he plopped his *Ace* on the *Queen of Trump* [♠] opening lead. Somehow, Somewhere, in the primeval past, Someone saved an ace, hid it in a bag of sand and used it to hit other players in the head. Since that time many civilized players harbor bitter feelings toward saving one's aces.

West apparently had this fear instilled in him from early on. Accordingly, he proceeded to reel off nine side aces, finishing with three *Aces of Diamonds*. East dutifully pitched a point on *'Seven of Nine'*. With 19 points in the bank, only one point was needed to set the contract. Since East played the *Jack* on the third *Ace of Diamonds*, West sniffed distinct possibilities for the 20th point and continued with the *King of Diamonds*.

Poof! East's *Ace of Diamonds* went up in smoke, as South ruffed in and led the *King of Spades* to pull the outstanding trumps. East should've given up the *Ace* to partner when the chance was there. Now North has the rest of the tricks. East soothed, *"Good try partner, sorry I had nothing to help you with."* Nothing but the *Ace of Diamonds* – if East had been counting – which would have made 20 HCP had East elected to pitch it on West's third *Ace of Diamonds*.

West's narrow view produced a swing of 130 points That's adding the 60 they should have made, to the 70 they allowed South to get away with. Maybe that's why the song says, *"19 is the loneliest number since the number One"*.

This hand appeared in my weekly Pinochle Passion column designed as a spoof on those who use the term *'sandbagger'*, a derogatory expression for players who do not play their aces the first time they have a chance. And to be fair, there are occasions when failure to play aces can result in losses.

However, the expert player has learned to differentiate between the occasions when aces must be cashed, or held up. How could this hand have been played differently, to get that one extra HCP that East/West so desperately needed here?

Upon a cursory examination of the hands it can be seen that there are ten top tricks available to the defense.

So, for a player holding ten aces there are two considerations. First, the possibility that Declarer's partner may trump one of my aces. Second, what holdings that I have can be maximized to produce additional tricks? Are there any tens that may develop as tricks?

Obviously the trump suit [♠] seems to offer the best opportunity for extra tricks. West holds a run in Declarer's suit. Is there a possibility of losing the *Ace of Trumps* if he does not take it right away? No, that can't happen since West has four spades to go with the ace.

There is also the possibility that West's partner may be able to get in on the trump lead. So very little incentive exists for West to run with the *Ace of Trumps* on the first lead while holding five trumps.

So, how does the play proceed differently, after West "Sandbags" on the first lead?

North wins with the *Ace of Trumps* [♠] and plays the *Ace of Hearts* and then the *Ace of Clubs*. Suppose North had the *Ace of Diamonds* instead of one of the other aces? Hey, 3 aces are THREE ACES. It's three tricks no matter how you count them. Which suit he takes them in is immaterial.

East/West still get their ten aces between them. Add to this the extra trump trick that West creates by the refusal to jump out the window on the first trump lead. There's just no way South should make this bid.

Play Your Aces, or Lose 'Em

Any more advice on playing aces? Why not! They always tell me, *"Play Your Aces!"* This is a caveat heralded loudly to all newcomers to the game. Old-timers smile knowingly even as they reap the benefits of this practice. "May it please the court, I wish to enter the next hand as evidence and to mark it as People's Exhibit # 1":

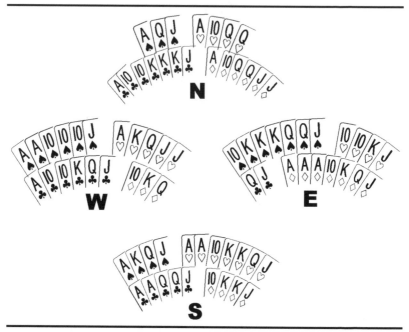

NORTH	EAST	SOUTH	WEST
51	52	60	Pass
Pass	Pass	Hearts	

Today's South intended to carry no *Aces* home and plunked down three outside *Aces* for a start. An attempt was then made to get across to partner. The *Queen of Trumps* [♥] was selected for this task.

West, a certified old-timer, stepped up with the *Ace of Hearts*, and showed that seniors too, know a thing or two about playing *Aces*. First one *Ace of Spades*, then the second *Ace* caused North to lose an *Ace,* left all alone now. West's *Ace of Clubs* was next, cut by East who was off to the races with three *Diamond Aces* and a *King of Diamonds* continuation. West gets a cut with the *Ten of Hearts* making 20 at this point. Looking around for gravy, West selects the *Ten of Clubs* for East to chomp on, snatching North's *Ace of Clubs* in the process.

By now, North is starting to wonder what's going on, meanwhile South has scrunched way down in the chair. For lack of a better play, East decides to let North in on the action with a spade cut. So they finally get the trumps pulled but West still gets the *Ten of Clubs* at the end for an undeserved 26 points to add to their 22 meld.

What a difference if South starts with trump [♥] instead of *Aces*. East/West still get all their *Aces* but have no way of saving, as 15 points are all they can make. East casts a knowing smile across to partner. They're not about to complain. North however, wants to know, *"What happened partner?"* South naturally, was duly affronted. *"What's the problem, I made my bid didn't I? Don't get so uptight Partner; it's just a game!"*

It's always nice to play a hand well. It leaves you with a warm fuzzy feeling as you drive away. But, what about the folks you left behind? It's highly possible that should East/West win the game, South will regret the missed opportunity to deny them those 48 points. Maybe the next time, South will think farther than just making the bid.

Saving Meld with Little Trump

This is another one of those 'Ray Charles' hands. Okay? While you rack up 90+ on this hand, what about the opponents?

Is there any way for them to save 46 points on this hand? Only one sure way, and today's bidder found it! As you will see, South has a blind spot involving his five losing spades.

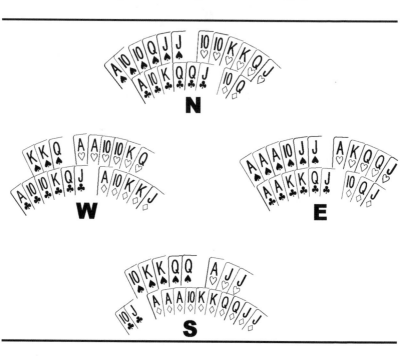

WEST	NORTH	EAST	SOUTH
50	51	Pass	60
65	Pass		70
Pass			Diamonds

Notice how this plays out so that East/West are still able to save Meld by getting the minimum 20 HCP.

South cashed the *Ace of Hearts* then plunked down the triple *Ace of Diamonds* and another trump.

West was waiting for him with two trump winners and exited with a heart. East cashed two clubs and gave South a club to ruff.

South belatedly realizes a disposal site is needed for those five losing spades. Too late! Good trump management often requires that necessary housekeeping chores be taken care of <u>before</u> trump is pulled.

South's best plan was leading spade losers at every chance. Second best plan would have been the lead of a small diamond at trick two, hoping to reach partner with the *Ten*.

Instead, South's approach forces West to turn trump winners instead of possibly using trump on books that partner has already won. Only an act of inspiration would move West to rise with the *Diamond Ten* to accomplish the same result.

East/West's best move of course, is to play the trump suit, the exact opposite of what South should be doing.

Confucius Say: "Both sides play same suit, One side Crazy!"

CHAPTER 10 - GET MORE FROM YOUR PARTNER
*"It's really hard playing against three people but I have a
regular partner, so I do it all the time!"*

Take a close look at the hand below and let's see why
our partner can be our best buddy, or worst enemy:

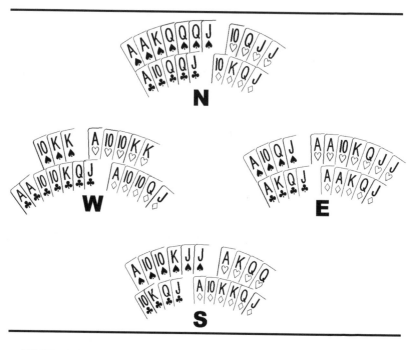

NORTH	EAST	SOUTH	WEST
52	54	60	65
Pass	Pass	70	Pass
		Diamonds	

Our hero South, finds himself at 70 without a clue on
where to pick up the 23 points he needs. His best chance at this
point is to hope his partner can cut his losers in spades before
the trumps are picked up. Failing that, maybe the opponents will
be forced to trump in.

Accordingly South leads out with the *Ace of Spades*, then the *King of Spades*. West cooperates with a pointer each time, and partner, **wonderful partner**, comes out with the second *Ace of Spades*. With no reason to revise partners lead, North continues with a third *Ace of Spades* and another spade.

West cuts with the *Jack of Trumps* and makes the good continuation of *King of Hearts* covered by the *Ten* and East's *Ace*.

A small heart comes back and South must step up with the *Ace* but gives no relief to the Defenders, instead dishing up another small spade for them to digest. West cringes as the *Ten* forces partner's *Ace of Trumps* [♦].

East can do no better than continue with the *Ace of Hearts* and another heart, putting partner in with the *Ace of Hearts*. West then provides the fifth heart for North and South to cut with the *King* and *Ten of Trumps* [♦].

The *Ten of Spades* in South's hand serves as a sacrifice as West cuts high with the *Ace of Diamonds* picking up the *King* from partner. West leads the *Queen of Clubs* next, taken by North's *Ace of Clubs;* followed with a *Queen of Trump* [♦] return forcing the *Ace from East*.

South, with the three outstanding *Trump Aces* [♦] out of the way, is more than willing to lose three clubs, enabling him to scamper home with 25 HCP's in his knapsack.

Dumping Trump – for Your Partner

All too often we see tremendous hands butchered because Declarer is trumping partner's winning cards. *"But that's the rules of the game"*, you say. *"Declarer must trump when holding no cards in the suit led."*

Well and good. Suppose Declarer has <u>no</u> trump, then what? *"Then they can't trump."*   Exactly! In those cases, Declarer must play off ALL the Trump, so as not to be in the way when partner's winners are rolled out. Meanwhile partner pitches any losing cards on the trumps.

Observe how this is demonstrated in the following hand:

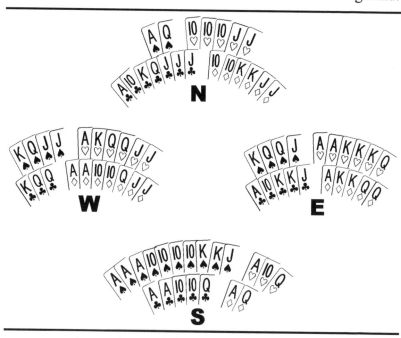

EAST	SOUTH	WEST	NORTH
52	54	60	65
Pass	Pass	Pass	Clubs

North starts out with the *Ace of Spades* on which South throws one of his three *Aces of Spades*. This is a special lead-back signal, which signifies that South is either trumping the suit or has control of the suit.

Also, South melded only 10 points after sending a 20 meld bid. This in itself should have alerted North to the fact that South was heavy with *Aces,* and that trump should have been taken out as soon as possible.

North is awake now and leads back, not another spade but a trump.

East rises with the *Ace of Clubs* and plays off his three other *Aces* (two *Hearts* and *Diamond*). An attempt is now made to cut the communications by playing another spade.

However South is up to the challenge and wins the *Spade Ace*. Two *Aces of Clubs* and the *Ten* are now played asking North to remove all trumps from the hands. After trumps are eliminated, North can reach South since South has carefully preserved an *Ace* in each suit as an entry to cash out the spade winners.

If East had not played *Aces* while in, their side would have lost two more tricks.

The lesson to be taken home is this: If your partner indicates he has a long side suit already established, get rid of your trump as early as possible. Once trump is out of the way, aces and tens in the side suits will take you a long way.

Dump Weak Side-Suits Before Drawing Trump

Trump management on the next hand involves much more than the strong trump suit, but includes the weak side suit hearts, which must be taken care of, before trump are drawn.

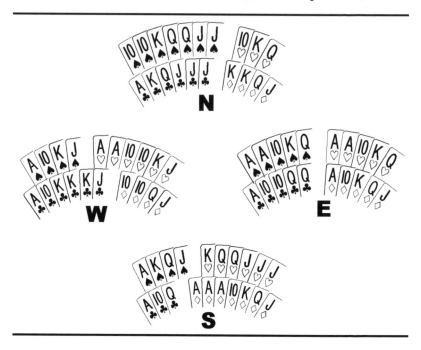

NORTH	EAST	SOUTH	WEST
52	55	60	Pass
Pass	70	75	
	Pass	Diamonds	

The 20-meld bid received from North with a subsequent meld of 28 indicates an extremely weak hand.

In addition, the show of aces and a run by RHO show a need to handle trump judiciously and avoid the loss of more than one trump trick if possible. It's good if opponents can be induced to use trumps on tricks that are already theirs.

Of course there remains the hope that North also can trump losing hearts.

#	North	East	South	West
1	Q♥	K♥	►Q♥	A♥
2	10♠	A♠	J♠	►K♠
3	K♦	►Q♦	A♦	J♦
South. Conceals holding triple aces				
4	K♥	10♥	►J♥	A♥
5	10♥	A♥	J♥	►K♥
West. {?} Trump lead better choice				
6	K♦	►J♦	10♦	Q♦
South. East is marked with the other ace				
7	J♦	Q♥	►Q♥	10♥
8	►J♣	Q♣	A♣	J♣
East. {?} Should play the ace and lead a trump				
9	Q♦	A♥	►K♥	10♥
10	►A♣	Q♣	10♣	K♣
North. Has done the damage and run				
11	►Q♠	A♠	Q♠	10♠
12	J♣	►A♦	J♦	10♦
13	K♣	►K♦	A♦	10♦
East. Trump lead too late, cow is already out of the barn.				
14	J♣	10♦	►J♥	J♥
15	Q♣	►A♣	Q♣	K♣
16	K♠	►10♣	Q♦	K♣
17	10♠	Q♠	►A♠	J♠
18	J♠	K♠	►K♠	A♠
19	J♠	10♣	K♦	►A♣
20	Q♠	10♠	►A♦	10♣
North/South make 29 HCP				

Defenders help Declarer by playing on hearts. They lost two tricks in hearts by not playing trump at every opportunity.

Often, with an expert Declarer, one can almost judge the right plays by doing the exact opposite of what he does. In this hand, when Declarer fails to start out with trump and leads the suit that West is strong in, West should be alerted to lead trump.

Also, since South melded a marriage in hearts and on the second heart lead, played the *Jack*, that signals at least three hearts in the South hand. All these indicators lead to the fact that South is trying to get his hearts trumped by someone. So always try to remember the meld and watch for those cards along with the other cards pitched by the Declarer.

Preserving Tempo

Tempo, in this context refers to the timing of a play or lead in a hand. Declarer may lose tempo when a play or lead is made out of the sequence in which it could be most effective.

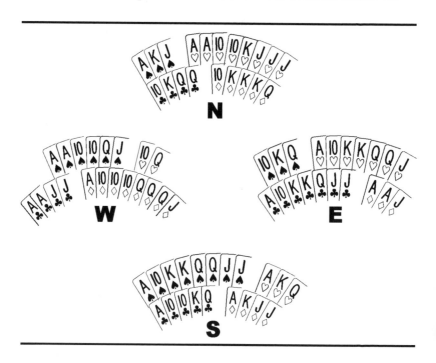

For example, when a stopper must be taken out or high trumps dislodged, the order in which it is done affects the tempo of the hand. For a Defender, gaining the tempo may mean attacking a stopper in Declarer's hand or taking out trump before Declarer's partner can use them to trump losers.

Follow the bidding for the hand already shown:

SOUTH	WEST	NORTH	EAST
55	Pass	56	60
70		Pass	Pass
Spades			

This is a typical rebid by Declarer, in that the hand must be evaluated twice. The first bid is made as a Responder where only meld and aces are counted. The hand has a value of 60 as support to a partner. Actual Meld counts aces 10, kings 8, marriages 8, double pinochle 30, plus 4 points for having at least four aces.

South actually shaved the meld by 10 points. I've heard this explanation more times than I can count; *"I figured if you couldn't do anything with 50 meld, then you would do no more if I sent you 60."*

North's response of 56 gave the impression that someone might have held a gun forcing the bid. In any case the point was moot, as South was not about to let North, East, West or a kibitzer take this bid without some serious haggling.

Let's follow the hand play to see how things develop:

Ace of Hearts was first on South's meeting agenda, then the *Ace of Diamonds*, followed by the ever popular *Queen of Trumps* [♠]. [*Survey rates this card as the # 1 choice of opening leads among expert players. -- That's the Queen of Trump , not necessarily the Queen of Spades.*]

West steps up to the podium with the *Ace of Trumps* [♠], then cashes the *Ace of Diamonds* noting with chagrin East's own fallen *Ace.* Nothing to do except change the strategy and continue with *Ten of Diamonds* to partner's fourth *Ace.* East plays *Ace of Hearts* and the *King,* as West trumps with the *Jack of Spades.* Back comes another *Ten of Diamonds* trumped by East with the *Queen of Spades.*

This time the *King of Hearts* bears scrutiny as South decides to run her *King of Trumps* [♠] through the West side of town. Oops, that mistake is snapped up with alacrity as West superimposes the *Ten of Trumps* [♠] on the trick. The *Queen of Diamonds* is now used to set up another trump trick for West as East trumps with the carefully preserved *Ten of Spades,* giving a resounding uppercut and forcing South's *Ace of Spades.* South has not lost sight of her original objective and uses this chance to push the trump again with what else, the *Queen of Spades.*

West is in a quandary. The original plan was to promote trump tricks. Now here's a trap. If the *Ace of Spades* is played and then the *Queen,* South can win the *Ten.* If instead the *Ten* is played, a trick is lost but the *Ace* is still held over South's *Ten.* Looking down at the diamonds West realizes that there are no more out, as 17 have been played. So, West plays the *Ace of Trump* [♠] picking up the *King* from North. West exits with the *Queen of Diamonds,* noting with satisfaction the *Ace* and *King of Trumps* [♠] from North and South.

This is the position after the twelfth book.

N

W

E

S

You can see that since North/South only have 9 HCP in the kitty so far, there's no way for them to pick up 11 more points with triple *Ace of Clubs* still out against them. The long *Diamonds* prove to be their undoing as West's relentless bombardment pumps South into submission.

Now that the hand has been played out, can you see a way it could have been made? An even more valuable lesson can be learned about what we call the tempo of the hand.

Often the Declarer will have several things to get done but the <u>*Order*</u> in which they are done is most important. This now becomes a Double Dummy problem where you get to look at all four hands and devise a solution to the problem.

What if South's first lead had instead been the *Queen of Trumps* [♠?] Yes, postpone the playing of aces until the trump situation is resolved. Make sense?

Now lay out the cards for exercise and play the hand out, as West takes the *Ace of Trump* [♠] then plays the *Ace of Diamonds* and then the *Ten* to East's *Ace of Diamonds*. East cashes the third *Ace of Diamonds* and then *Ace of Hearts* getting out with the *Queen of Hearts*.

South is in with the *Ace of Hearts* and pushes the *Ace of Spades* and then the *Jack*. West plays the *Queen of Spades* which is won by North.

North now plays the *Ace of Hearts* which goes around to West's *Ten of Trump* [♠]. A small diamond exit comes back to South with the *Ace of Diamonds*. South's *Queen of Clubs* disposes of one of West's club stoppers and another diamond is led for South to trump.

The *King of Clubs* knocks out another club stopper from West and the diamond return has South trumping again. South leads the *Ten of Clubs* next to East's *Ace* with a heart return, trumped small by South with West over-ruffing.

West leads another diamond ruffed by South with the *Ten*. South now plays the *Ace of Clubs* and the fifth club which West ruffs with the *Ten of Trumps* [♠] for his last trick.

What difference do you note? The <u>Major</u> <u>Difference</u>? South makes 22 HCP despite brilliant defense.

The lesson to be learned? Stick to the plan. Do not get sidetracked along the way, and hope that your partner also does not deviate.

On this hand South had a lot to get done. Four winners in trump and three club stoppers had to be knocked out. Also the bonus for last trick had to be secured before Declarer could rest. As long as the heart and diamond aces were held, tempo was preserved. You saw that defenders were required to knock out both diamond and heart stoppers before they could start the bidder trumping.

On the previous play Declarer was ripe for the picking, since she had already opened up for the ruffs by getting rid of her stoppers first. Of course it goes without saying that one's partner must be in synch for all this to occur. If they do not continue our objective but instead get busy playing aces, they take away the tempo and allow our aces to be trapped.

Don't Change Horses Mid-stream

An old adage sometimes holds true in Pinochle. *"Don't change horses in mid-stream."*

South had two ways to play this next hand. One, play on hearts to use up the opponents trumps while holding stoppers in the side suits. Second, draw trump and make partners aces good. South understandably decided to try drawing the trump after seeing partner show aces in the meld.

Unfortunately, North changed direction and pursued a different course for no apparent reason. And of course, South had no way of knowing what was going through partner's mind. We mentioned before that one's partner must continue the tempo that Declarer has set, for it to succeed.

This hand shows what can happen if that rule is ignored.

SOUTH	WEST	NORTH	EAST
50	51	54	55
56	Pass	Pass	60
65			Pass
Clubs			

Follow along with the play of the cards and see where things begin to go wrong. If partner maintained the tempo set by Declarer, things could have turned out much better.

#	North	East	South	West
1	A♣	J♣	▶Q♣	K♣
2	▶A♠	J♠	10♠	J♠
3	▶A♠	Q♠	10♠	J♠
4	▶A♥	J♥	10♥	J♥
5	▶A♥	Q♥	Q♥	10♥
6	▶A♦	J♦	10♦	J♦

Failing to return a trump at trick 2, the last chance to put the plan back on track, was by playing a trump here. Follow the rest of the play to see the results of North's decision not to follow South's tactics as outlined by the initial trump lead.

#	North	East	South	West
7	▶Q♠	K♠	A♠	J♠
North. {??} Stick to partners plan, return trumps!				
8	Q♣	A♣	▶J♣	K♣
9	J♥	▶10♥	J♥	J♣
10	Q♠	Q♣	A♠	▶K♠
11	J♦	▶A♦	Q♦	K♦
East/West. Making their trumps separately!				
12	Q♦	▶A♦	10♦	Q♦
13	K♦	▶10♦	A♦	10♣
14	K♠	J♦	K♣	▶Q♠
Trump lead by North at 2nd trick would have avoided this!				
15	K♥	K♥	▶Q♥	10♣
16	K♣	K♥	Q♣	▶A♣
17	K♦	Q♦	10♣	▶J♣
18	K♥	A♥	▶Q♥	K♠
19	10♥	▶10♦	A♣	10♠
20	K♦	A♥	▶10♣	10♠

Had North returned the trump at trick 2, the hand plays altogether differently, and East/West do not save their meld. North saw that South played no aces, opting to remove trump. North counts six aces in his hand plus any that South has not yet played. This should tell North that the only danger to this hand would be in allowing the defense to ruff good tricks with worthless trump. North should stick with South's plan to remove trump and avoid losing the 50+ points saved by East/West.

"Start of a Lasting Partnership"

Head Rub, Anyone?

Some of this stuff you just can't make up, I witnessed this next Head Rub personally. [A Head Rub is a regional penalty for allowing a Trickless.] It Was Not Pretty! I am glad to say I was not on the receiving end of it!

East felt good as he picked up his hand, a strong two-suiter capable of pulling at least 30 plus in HCP. South was perspiring, as the last three cards she picked up were heart tens. That is enough to make the bottom of your stomach drop out, but you get over it!

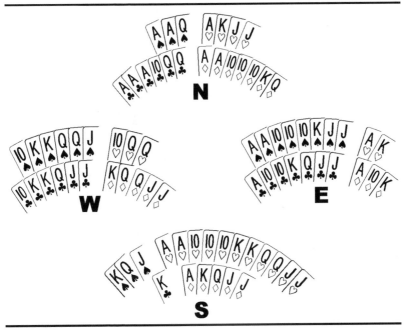

EAST	SOUTH	WEST	NORTH
50	65	80	Pass
85	100	Pass	
110	120		
Pass	Hearts		

No need to fool around when you have a double run, South bids 65 with hers. West tried to make it interesting, but how can you fight a double run, unless you have one too? Add in the possibility of a *Head Rub*, and nothing else is material.

South knew she could reach partner with a heart, but the thought of picking up East's *Ace of Hearts* was also tantalizing. So just for insurance, South cashed her two *Heart Aces*.

With the fall of East's *Ace of Trumps*, it was now 'Lock City'! South first cashed the *Ace of Diamonds* to clarify the situation for partner. A heart continuation put North in and the last heart was returned.

The fact that North cashed no outside *Aces* made it apparent that she had controls in all suits ahead of East. Had North been unsure about a suit she would cash that *Ace* first, so South would know not to return in that suit. In this case South had no reservations in getting rid of every trump in her hand.

North pitched losers down tight to seven *Aces* and the *Ten of Diamonds*. When South finally got out with a diamond, every card in North's hand was good since East's *Ace of Diamonds* fell on the third round.

Each of the ladies came over to rub his head, (the traditional penalty in some circles for allowing a Trickless to be run against you) and East quipped: *"Ladies Luck!"* He's right, but they still have to know how to read it, and most importantly, how to play it!

Knocking Out Stoppers

This is an advanced theme and requires that you lay out the cards to benefit from the points being made. So it would be good at this point to separate the cards into suits, lay out each hand and follow card by card as it is played. We will show how Declarer and Defenders can each benefit from knocking out key cards in the opposing hands.

When basketball first became popular, many kids were too lazy to run up and down the court. They would often stay on their end of the court, wait for teammates to rebound and throw the ball back for an easy lay-up. We called them 'pot-hangers'.

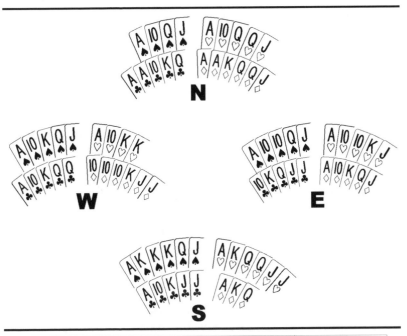

SOUTH	WEST	NORTH	EAST
52	53	55	Pass
56	Pass	Pass	
Spades			

East/West elected to hang around the pot and wait for something to be thrown to them. South decided to make Spades trump, feeling it was a tad stronger than the hearts because of the triple kings. After playing the *Ace of Diamonds*, South reached out to remove trumps if possible, selecting the *Queen of Spades* {?}. [Perhaps the *King of Spades* was a better choice for knocking out West's stopper.]

West made a good play at this point by covering with the *King of Spades* and North was in with the *Ace,* cashing double *Ace of Diamonds* and returning the *Queen of Trumps* [♠.]

East's *Ten of Trumps* forces South's *Ace.* [Working on South's stopper now.] South persists with *Jack of Spades* (no better play,) and West lets it run to East's *Ace. King of Hearts* takes out South's heart stopper. South leads *Queen of Hearts* covered by a *King* and North's *Ace.* North comes back with the *Jack of Hearts* covered by *Ten* and West's *Ace.*

West now pulls the trump [♠] with an *Ace* and *Ten*, then leads the *Ten of Diamonds* to remove South's last trump. South leads the *Queen of Hearts* hoping to clear hearts while retaining a club stopper. East's lead of the *Ten of Clubs* knocks out South's stopper in clubs dashing South's hopes for further entry.

The next play will either lock out the pot hangers, or allow for profit sharing. South passively leads the *Jack of Clubs* {?}, (*King* is no better, *Ten* is the only killing lead, effectively shutting down the defense). West retains his stopper and simply covers with the *Queen of Clubs* allowing North to win with the *Ten*. North may try a heart play, but East then puts North right back in with a club. If North should now try a diamond, East would simply play a club toward West with the *King of Clubs* covered by the *Ten* and *Ace*, to cash another diamond for the 53 point save.

Were you able to see, how at different points throughout the hand, both offense and defense had an opportunity to knock out stoppers? Moral: When defenders leave a pot hanger down-court, leave a man there to cover him.

Coping with Meld-itus

As I may have mentioned, I started writing this book while confined in the hospital. On the adjacent Hospital ward, I met South, a patient suffering from a social disease, Melditus.

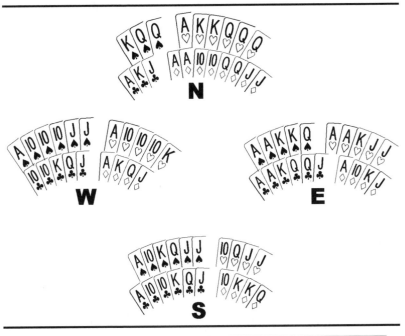

EAST	SOUTH	WEST	NORTH
52	53	Pass	54
65	70		Pass
Pass	Clubs		

Melditus is easily diagnosed as the symptoms are readily apparent, even to the layman. Patient wakes up with a weak hand and goes outside without sufficient covering. Large blotches of meld show up on partners legs and arms. Patient attempts to carry this heavy load of meld, hoping for help from defenders. This disease can cause temporary loss of breath and brain damage, leading to cardiac arrest if not resuscitated by helpful opponents. Just watch.

South has not a prayer of making 20 HCP on this hand without some serious help from all three of the other players. Distribution of the hand is too flat, and there is no long suit to run. However we give South credit for formulating a scheme that may fool at least one defender into assisting, if partner at least cooperates with the plan.

South wants to allow partner to trump one or two losing spades but does not want to make it obvious by leading the *Ace of Spades* and another. Therefore the very sneaky lead of the *Queen of Spades* {!}, **Trick 1**.

West decides to jump out the window with the *Ace* on the first round and then looks around for new worlds to conquer. Right away South gets help in making this bid, as West starts taking off all his clothes, (Shedding all his stoppers in the side suits.) West plays off *Ace of Hearts*, **Trick 2**, and *Ace of Diamonds*, **Trick 3**. This now places the entire burden of the defense on the unwitting partner, East.

It suddenly occurs to West that North may be able to trump a spade or two if allowed to keep any trumps. So West belatedly plays a trump, the *Queen of Clubs* {?.} How much better to have played the trump while retaining the side suit stoppers. And even now, while playing trump is a good idea, why not make an attacking lead of the *King of Clubs* or *Ten* to knock out a stopper in trump, instead of the pathetic *Queen*? In any case, North wisely retains the *Ace* and pushes East off one of his stoppers in trump with the *King of Clubs*, **Trick 4**.

East now has a dilemma. [How nice it <u>would have been</u> at this point, to be able to push the *King of Hearts* and pick up the *Ten* from South as a counter for partner.] Alas, West has already sold the team's birthright by playing *Ace of Hearts* on nothing. As it stands, the lead of the *Queen of Clubs* seems to be a good possibility. South covers with the *King of Clubs* forcing West's *Ten* to North's *Ace* (***Trick 5***). [3 HCP for North/South]

North now assesses how to might make the maximum contribution to the <u>Cause</u>. ['Cause' he wants to save his meld!] Accordingly North removes another stopper from East by playing the *Ten of Diamonds*, ***Trick 6***.

East does not know the exact situation in diamonds but reasons that it must be good to cut communication lines by continuing with them, so at ***Trick 7*** he returns a diamond which rides around to North's *Ten*. [Up to 5 HCP for North/South] Everyone now knows the diamond situation, so North must knock out a heart stopper while retaining a heart entry. Plays *Queen of Hearts* to East's *Ace*, ***Trick 8***. East returns another *Queen of Trumps* [♣] won by South, ***Trick 9***. [North/South now have 6 HCP.] South attempts to knock out another stopper by leading a spade covered by West's *Ten* and won by East, ***Trick 10***. East continues with the last diamond won by North, ***Trick 11***. [9 HCP for North/South at this point]

North uses the last chance to pull trump by playing a small diamond ruffed by East with the *King* and over-ruffed by South's *Ten*, with West contributing a *King*, ***Trick 12***. [12 HCP for North/South] South plays a spade to knock out East's last stopper at this point as West's *Ten* forces the *Ace*, ***Trick 13***.

Here is East's last time at bat. Here the *Heart Ace* should have been played and a heart returned to knock out North's last stopper. Instead East returns the *Queen of Spades* which South wins with the *Ace*! [***Trick 14***, and 14 HCP]

This was disingenuous, as South wanted to give the impression that West held the remaining two *Tens*. South now cashes the *Ace of Clubs*, ***Trick 15***, with North pitching the *King of Hearts* for 17 HCP. South plays the last club, North pitching a diamond and East is helpless, ***Trick 16***. If East now plays a spade, (which is tempting) East/West make no more tricks as North plays the *Queen of Hearts* on South's *Ten of Spades*, for 29 HCP. If instead East cashes the *Ace of Hearts*, North wins the last three tricks to make 27 HCP. Whereas, if East gives up a heart first, they split the HCP 25/25.

Where did East/West go wrong? At least seven times. ***Trick 1.*** West can let the first spade go through to East who returns a club. Failing that, if West takes the first trick, play the *King* or *Ten of Clubs* at ***Trick 2***, knocking out a North entry. Or missing that, then at ***Trick 3***, West can lead any heart, which knocks out North's heart entry. One last chance for West came at ***Trick 4***, when he could have knocked out North's heart entry. East also had opportunities at ***Tricks 5***, ***8***, and ***10*** to play a heart dislodging North's stopper.

Despite all the help from opponents, we give South credit for the original plan and revisions. Since the spade ruff plan was not working, South changed to set up the spade suit, because of having retained a stopper in that suit originally. North too gets credit for helping to establish the diamond suit. All in all, North/South gave themselves every opportunity to save by playing to knock out the opposing stoppers.

As a result of this and other case histories, Medical Science has now perfected a cure for Melditus that has proven to be 90% effective. Helpful Opponents! Now friends, that last hand <u>was</u> Rocket Science and <u>this</u> is why they often refer to me as the Doctor!

Dummy Reversal

Dummy Reversal is an expert skill known in the Bridge world, where a bidder's trump are used to cut side suits while partner's trump suit is used to pick up the Defender's trump. Perhaps North was a former Bridge player, which may have led him to take this circuitous route on the attached hand:

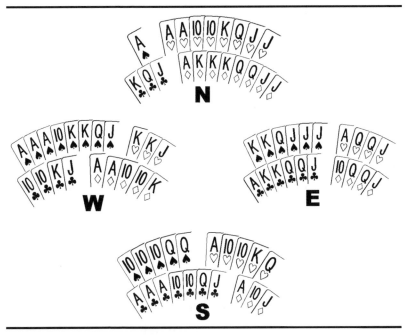

EAST	SOUTH	WEST	NORTH
52	53	65	70
Pass	Pass	Pass	Hearts

Ace of Spades opens, followed by the *Queen of Hearts*. East wins and plays the *Jack of Spades*. North ruffs with the *King of Trumps* [♥] and leads the *Queen of Clubs*. East wins the *Ace* and lets North ruff another spade with the *Ten*. A club lead is taken by South and a spade is ruffed by North with the *Ten*.

South takes the third club and leads another spade to be ruffed with the *Ace*. The *Ace of Diamonds* and another diamond to South's *Ace*. South picks up all hearts and leads club winners, giving up a diamond at next to last trick. Note that North ruffing high allows him to under-lead and put South in with the trumps.

Readers taking the time to lay out the hand will discover that it plays 2 points better with the reversal, than with conventional methods. Check it out, maybe one day you might need those 2 points.

Disney's Not So Wonderful World

If you ever get a chance to play with Larry S. from Orlando, FL., get him to tell you about this hand he played in NYC. Larry was the dealer picking up his hand last and looking for a little help, these were his first 17 cards:

Larry is of course, now squeezing each card painfully in an effort to extract maximum sympathy for his <u>cause</u>. ('Cause' he wants a double run!) His last three cards were the *Ace of Diamonds*, then the *Ace of Hearts*, finally, another *Ace of Diamonds*! Meanwhile the players are bidding in front of him.

When the bid comes around, Larry's Right Hand Opponent bids 150! Larry passes without a second thought, and the player lays down a double run in spades.

As Larry watches the meld go down, that's when it hits Larry ***THAT HE TOO HAS A DOUBLE RUN, <u>WITH ACES</u>!!*** Larry can't say anything, but the other players sense something is wrong when his eyes bulge out, sweat begins to pop out on his face, and he starts to roll around on the floor. I'm sure you get the picture! Again, It Was Not A Pretty Sight!

To this day, if Larry starts to rack up a lot of diamonds in his hand, he does not trust himself to finish picking up the hand. I call it Longemaniphobia. Fear of a Long Diamond Hand.

PART 4 - FOR THE DEFENSE

CHAPTER 11 - DEFENSIVE STRATEGIES
*"Pinochle unlike Bridge, has no dummy hand.
By the way, have you met my partner yet?"*

Unless you are one of the world's best cardholders (always get good hands,) about half of your card playing career will be spent defending against someone else's bid. Therefore, a large portion of your attention should be directed to getting as much as possible out of those hands.

We think defense should be simple. One, you don't have the pressure of the bid, so you don't have as much to lose if you go wrong. Two, you are reacting to Declarer's moves since he gets to start the hand. So basically, we have reduced defense to two main positions. One is where you have Power, (*Aces*) the other is where the offense has the Power.

Do You have any Power?
Let's look at examples, some where you have the Power and others where you may not.

Sample 11a:
Spades are trump. Declarer melds a double marriage in clubs and jacks and you hold the following:

You Have the POWER! and you need to get rid of the trump so your clubs will be good. In this hand if no one trumps your clubs, you will turn at least four club tricks.

***Sample 11b*:**

How about a second one. Spades are still trump. Responder, (bidders' partner) melds a double marriage in clubs with jacks around. Indications are that your partner was coming in clubs. You hold the clubs below:

A A A 10 Q J J J ♣

You Do NOT have the Power! On this hand you will be fortunate to turn one club, as Declarer has no clubs and will surely be trumping them.

***Sample 11c*:**

Spades are trump (spades are always trump, right?) Declarer has melded a pinochle, a run, roundhouse and jacks for 43 points. Responder melds double pinochle, jacks and three side suit marriages for 40 points after sending a 30 jump bid.

Your Hand:

Declarer plays the *Ace of Diamonds* and continues with the *Queen of Clubs* to your partners *Ten*. You have POWER! Your partner has Power. Responder has nothing. He couldn't even send his full meld because his hand was too weak. If the hand is played properly, the opposition is going DOWN.

The formula for Power is in this simple mnemonic: **ACESPOT**. Explanation? Anytime you and your partner have <u>ACES</u> to make, <u>P</u>lay <u>O</u>ut <u>T</u>rump!

On defense as well as offense, whenever you have <u>Aces</u> To Make, no question you better, oughta, <u>P</u>lay <u>O</u>ut <u>T</u>rump! If you don't, someone is going to trump your good tricks.

Review our 3 examples to see how this applies. On hand (*11a*) you know Declarer has those clubs to lose. You have the Power, and Aces To Make. Play Out the Trump!

On hand (*11b*) where you Do Not have the Power and you know Declarer will be trumping clubs? Now, **NOPALS** - <u>P</u>lay <u>A</u> <u>L</u>ong <u>S</u>uit. Make Declarer use up his trumps and hopefully lose control of the hand.

What about the third example? You have the Power and <u>Aces</u> To Make. You must <u>P</u>lay <u>O</u>ut <u>T</u>rump. As soon as partner wins the *Ten of Clubs*, he should switch to a trump. You will put in the ten to force out Declarer's *Ace*. When you regain the lead, push the *King of Trumps* [♠] through Declarer to try and get all the trump off the board. So, we sum up defense with:

ACESPOT - ACES To Make? Play Out Trump.
NOPALS - No Power? Play A Long Suit.

We welcome Declarer trumping our long suit; we love to see those trumps used up. Just make sure there's no help from the bidder's partner, don't let that turkey into the act. [Unless both of them are trumping the same suit.]

We also don't want our partner to use up trumps ruffing our good tricks. Why should our partner ruff tricks that already belong to us? If he gets rid of his trumps, he can then throw counters on our winners. And of course when he plays off his trumps, he is taking Declarer's trumps with him also.

When trumps are in three hands, Declarer, Responder, and yours, if you play a trump you pull <u>two</u> for every <u>one</u> you play. Here's how it looks (after six tricks have been played):

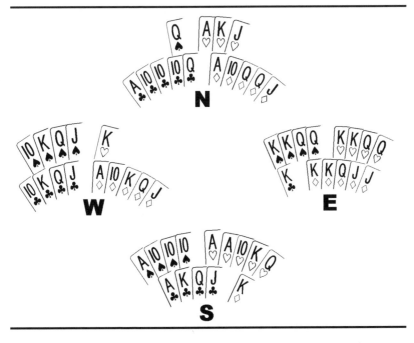

East won the bid making Diamonds trump.

You have the lead as North. You Must Lead Trumps Right Away! Else, West gets to trump hearts while East trumps clubs. Also You will be trumping spades, your partner's suit. Which trump do you lead? The *Jack*! Next time, the *Queen*! After that you can pick up two rounds with your *Ace/Ten*.

How about this scenario?

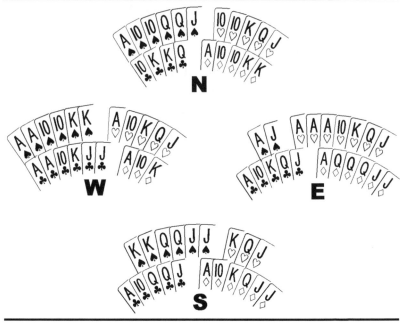

WEST	NORTH	EAST	SOUTH
52	Pass	60	70
Pass		75	80
		Pass	Diamonds

With South looking at 61 points in his own hand, East is seriously outgunned. However, trying to bring back 20 HCP will be no picnic with both opponents showing aces around.

South cashes the *Ace of Clubs* and gets off on the good foot by starting the spade suit. West ducks the first spade. North gets in and dutifully continues spades to East with the *Ace.*

Here is the **_last chance_** to set the hand. If East starts South trumping hearts, South will be happy to trump the hearts and let East trump the spades, getting away with 20 points. East sees no point in trumping partner's spade tricks and accordingly begins to divest the trump, leading the *Queen of Diamonds.*

South lets the first one go by, West wins and continues with the *Ten of Trump* [♦]. North wins and pushes spades again. East trumps in, cashes the *Ace of Trump* [♦] and pushes the fifth trump. South wins and perseveres with spades taken by East's last trump. West's two spades are still good and ***now*** the hearts go to work. South must trump the fourth and fifth hearts and North trumps the sixth heart losing two clubs at the end. North/South make 16 points, no more.

Always be leery of a Declarer who doesn't pull your trump and is willing to let you cut up tricks. Maybe you are cutting your partner's tricks. Consider getting rid of your trump so you can throw counters on partner's tricks.

Partner's Aces can Kill You

Any of you who are old enough, may recall an episode from the TV drama "DRAGNET".

"This is the City, Los Angeles California. Me and my partner Frank Smith., were working the day watch of the homicide division in the Upper Crust. We got a call reporting a suspicious death in the Country Club card room. When we arrived nothing had been moved and the witnesses were still at the table. A little old lady watched us come in and started shaking. I'm a cop. My name's Friday."

"Who actually witnessed the incident, all we want are the facts"? I asked.

"I was the Declarer", piped up the little old lady.

"Would you mind showing me some ID?" I watched as she whipped out a long plastic folder full of credit cards. *"How about something with your picture on it?"* She had two library cards and an International Kibitzers Card. *"Enough, show me the evidence!"*

I didn't need to wait for a post-mortem. They pulled back the sheet. This was the hand lying on the table:

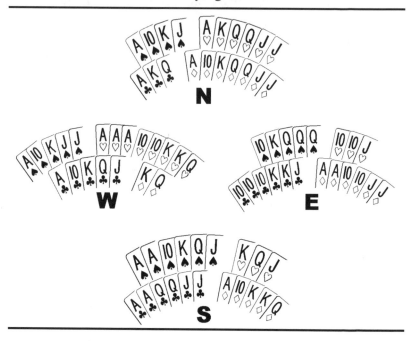

WEST	NORTH	EAST	SOUTH
51	53	Pass	60
70	Pass		75
Pass			Spades

I sniffed the hand; it was already starting to stink. *"How did the play go?"* She said she needed 26 HCP, so she cashed her three outside aces.

"What about the Spades?" Frank asked.

*"**Of course I played my aces!**"* she snorted. *"**Then I attempted to reach my partner.**"*

"Don't tell me," I opined, *"your partner's Ace of Clubs got caught, he had to use his Trump Ace to cut with, you wound up cutting his Ace of Hearts, you got set, and the opponents saved!"*

*"**How did you know?**"* she gasped.

"Just a lucky guess Ma'am, but you definitely killed this hand."

*"**How's that?**"* she asked.

I pulled the sheet back over the table. *"You killed it with your Aces, Ma'am. Read 'er her rights, Frank."*

She started to tear up, *"**How should I have played it?**"*

"Probably as a kibitzer, then I'm sure you would have seen everything!"

In less than a week, she was back on the streets. Found incompetent to stand trial. She still plays at the club, but they don't call us anymore. No point.

Don't Lose Meld Trying to Set Your Opponent

Sometimes you get carried away when someone comes in your best suit and you start thinking about setting them, when you should be thinking about saving your meld. North found to his chagrin, that it might not be as easy as it looked.

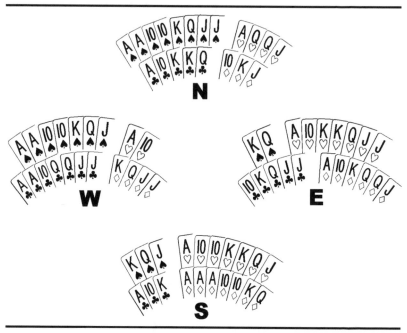

SOUTH	WEST	NORTH	EAST
50	51	Pass	54
65	70		Pass
Pass	Spades		

West played double *Ace of Clubs* and *Ace of Hearts*, then made a fantastic lead of the *King of Diamonds*. Like looking through the backs of the cards. East played the *Ace of Diamonds* and *Ace of Hearts,* then returned a diamond which South won with the *Ten*. [Only 2 HCP so far.]

At this point South made the technical mistake of cashing the *Ace of Clubs* [4 HCP] then the *Ace of Hearts*. Best defense would have been to retain the club stopper to serve as an entry for pushing the hearts and forcing West to trump.

Anyway, West trumps with the *King of Spades* and continues with another club making South trump partner's good trick. [6 HCP]

Instead of getting rid of the useless trump now, South routinely pushes another heart. Best would have been the *Queen of Spades* pushing West into North's strength, who showed a trump run in the meld.

West must ruff again and now lets South ruff another of North's club winners. [7 HCP] This time when South pushes the heart, West trumps with the *Ten* pushing North off an *Ace*. [10 HCP] North gets out with his last diamond. Again, not the best choice since it opens one up to ruffing. Best was the *Queen of Trump* [♠] to force a *Ten* from West.

South wins the *Ace of Diamonds* [11 HCP] then plays a heart ruffed by West with the *Ace of Trumps*. Back comes the *Ten of Clubs* which North attempts to win cheaply with the *Spade Queen. East* over-ruffs. A diamond return finds North ruffing with the *Spade King.* [13 HCP thus far] North with only spades left, is now forced to play a spade into West.

[Had North ruffed with the *Jack of Trump* instead of the *King* on this trick, they salvage 20 HCP exactly!]

Here is the situation after Trick 16:

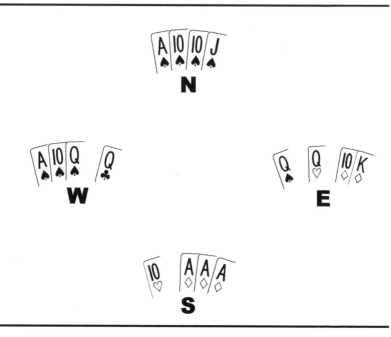

If now North leads the *Ten of Spades*, they are in the playoffs with 23 HCP. Alas! he sent the *Jack* to do a **Man's** job! West won with the *Ten* and sent out the *Queen of Clubs*.

North won and gave up a *Ten* to take the last trick, but only scrounged up 18 HCP on a hand where they should split the deck at least. A Sad State of Affairs!

Mrs. Throckmorton at the Sanitarium

Often you see real talent, and do your best to cultivate it, but at times your efforts may not be appreciated. Mrs. Evelyn Throckmorton, chairperson of the Ladies Auxiliary, Whitfield Sanitarium, takes her group on monthly visits to the institution.

On one visit she saw four tables of inmates playing Pinochle. She was advised that recent attraction to the game was due to Mr. Martin, an inmate recently transferred in from another State Institution, who had begun teaching the game.

Observing him for a few hands she realized that he was indeed a virtuoso. She asked to speak to Mr. Martin in private and was advised that this was not wise since he was committed for violence in the past. Of course she insisted and was reluctantly allowed to speak with him in the garden. She was warned to say nothing that would threaten his Pinochle playing.

She asked Mr. Martin if he would be willing to accept a salaried position teaching Pinochle at her club if she had him released. Mr. Martin was elated at the prospect and promised to cooperate with any efforts made in his behalf. Mrs. Throckmorton promised that at the next meeting of the Board, she would apply for his parole into her custody.

As she turned to leave the garden Martin spied a loose cobblestone, which he quickly picked up and hurled at her retreating form. It caught her a glancing blow behind the ear bringing her to her knees with blood streaming down her neck.

She turned to see him standing quietly, smiling all the while. *"How could you?"* She gasped, *"I was going to get you released!"*

He nodded, ***"Yes, I know. I just wanted to make sure you don't forget! OK?"***

CHAPTER 12 - PICKING UP COUNTERS
"Winners say: 'Nice hand partner,'
Losers say: 'Deal the cards!'"

Because we know much more about defending now, we can start experimenting. See how you do with this next hand which should test your powers of recollection.

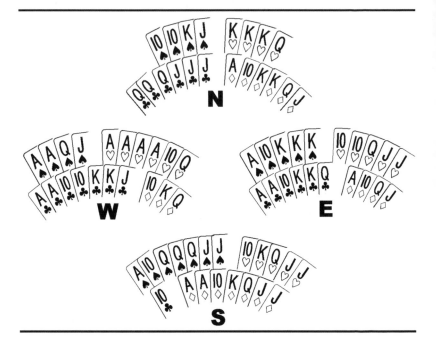

SOUTH	WEST	NORTH	EAST
50	Pass	Pass	Pass
Diamonds			

We've played this hand before, let's not have the same results. South started trumps right away by leading the *Queen of Diamonds*. [We're West this time around.]

Remember, North melded a run and will win this trick. So play the *Ten of Diamonds*. Next time we get in, the *King of Diamonds* may win an extra point for us when we push it. North wins with the *Ace of Diamonds* and returns the trump.

This time, East's *Ten* forces South's *Ace* and South now starts hearts. We win, [2 HCP] then lead our *King of Clubs*. East is in with the *Ace* [5 HCP]. East returns the *King of Spades* won by South with the *Ace*. South plays another heart which we win [8 HCP] and return the *Ace of Clubs*. South trumps and plays another heart. We win [10 HCP] and return a trump.

Having gotten rid of our *Ten* we are now able to push the *King of Trumps* [♦] to pick up a three pointer. East wins the *Ace* [13 HCP] and returns his other *King of Spades*. This is another three-bagger [16 HCP] that we win with the *Ace*. We return another club. South trumps in and plays another heart that we win [19 HCP].

We cash the other *Ace of Spades* [22 HCP] and return the spade won by East with the *Ace* [24 HCP]. East plays his last trump. So whatever North is able to contribute in assistance, at least we took as many trumps off the board as possible. We give up another club for South to trump.

South returns a small heart trumped by North. North's club return knocks out South's last trump. South is left with three small spades. North can trump one with his last trump, but the last two tricks are ours for 30 HCP. Well deserved I must say. Are you not much prouder of this defense?

Words from the Wise

No chapter on defense would be complete without words from the Old Masters of the game. Their gems of wisdom echo down through the ages and their play provides guideposts for all who strive to emulate their skill.

The next hand was taken directly from the Old Master file in the Library of Congress.

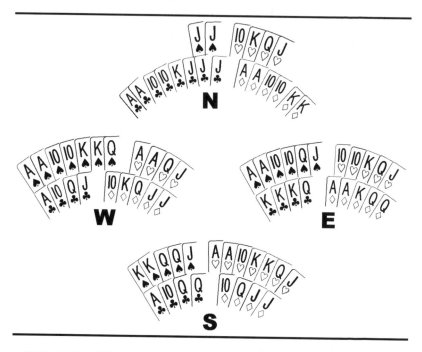

NORTH	EAST	SOUTH	WEST
Pass	50	60	Pass
	Pass	Hearts	

An old Pinochle Master told me: "*When I count up and see we made 20, I'm grateful. But if I find we made 30, then I'm mad!*" I wanted to know why.

He explained: *"If we made 20 we must have struggled hard for it, so naturally I am grateful. But if we only made 30, we probably missed a point somewhere, and the opponents are the ones who should be grateful!"*

On this hand, East/West had a chance to be grateful and make South mad at the same time. For some obscure reason South chose *Queen of Clubs* as an opening lead. West jumped on the *Ace* and reeled off double *Aces in Spades*. After receiving ace on ace from partner, West continued spades and was mildly surprised to see North take a bite out of the crime.

North looked at the meld and saw South lay down four spades. [Pity poor West, who saw the same meld but dismissed it from thought.] Looking for a way to sneak into the South hand for another munchie, North hit upon the lead of the *Jack of Clubs*. South dutifully finessed the *Ten* and produced another spade for partner to trump. North could see no better than another club underlead as South was surely marked with the *Ace*. South's fifth spade was then disposed of in the same fashion. North properly returned the last trump.

It was now a mere formality to force out West's high trump. South was then able to pitch the diamond losers on the established clubs after playing out all the trump.
Score: 57 Meld + 36 HCP = 93 points total.

If South pushes spades from the beginning; West would have surely been alerted that South was trying to get the losers trumped. West could then have led a low heart forcing South's *Ace*. On the next spade lead West could clear out the trump and turn all five of South's spades, saving meld in the process. Hopefully South was grateful for the lapse. The Old Master would have been.

When Aces Get You No Extra HCP (Counters)

Another hand from the file in Washington. This Old Master was out on the West coast and had been invited to play at one of those posh clubs up in the foothills of L.A.

A mild mannered Pakistani named Yusaf was running the valet service. His warm greeting followed the generous tip and he promptly disappeared with the car. Entering the club, the master was ushered into the elegantly appointed Game Room and found succulent pickings at the hors d'oeuvres table.

The luck of the draw paired him with a gentleman who was congenial but didn't seem to know much about the game. The hands were nondescript and the score was pretty even when he was dealt this hand in the South position.

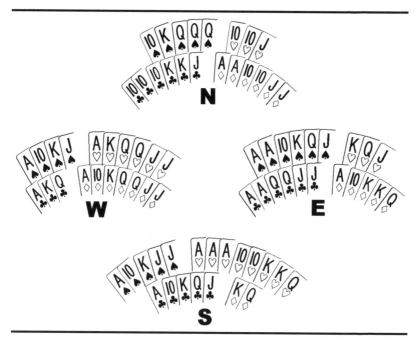

The bidding proceeded as follows:

SOUTH	WEST	NORTH	EAST
51	53	Pass	60
70	Pass		75
Pass			Spades

In his own words: *"I opened with a 51 in case my partner had a run. Not that my suit was shabby, but I was missing the jack and all."*

West sent 20 meld and this lady on my right took off like a rocket. I figured I'd boost the ante and bid her up a little bit, so she ended up at 75 needing 26. I couldn't see where she had a problem since her partner had aces around.

Right away, she started popping her aces like they were sugar pills. She played five of them including two aces of trump before she stopped and took a breath. Then she came out with another trump.

I wasn't planning to take any of my aces home so I went right up with my *Ace*. I knew my hearts were gonna get chopped up so I played the *Ace of Clubs* before I started the hearts. My eyes kinda popped when West slammed his *Ace of Clubs* down after mine and glared at his partner.

"Well," I thought, *"that's their problem."* I started my hearts going and churned out three aces with everybody still in the mix. I figured no harm in trying another one and my *King of Hearts* brought North's *Ace*.

It was awesome when my partner ruffed in with the *Ten* and choked off the lady who could only follow with a small trump since she had already played off her aces.

My partner laid down his *Ace of Diamonds* and got out with a club so West had to cut with his *Ace of Trumps* [♠].

He was already fuming at his partner, so when he laid down his *Ace of Diamonds* and I cut it, he really hit the roof. All the time she was just looking, like '*What's the matter?*'

I was counting and saw we had 19, so I went ahead and played my *Ten of Trumps* [♠] for 20 plus HCP. I got out with the *Queen of Hearts*, which took out her last trump, so I was surprised when she came right back with a club.

Of course my *Ten* stood up, and like I said there were no more trumps, so all my hearts were good after that.

We made 33 on the hand, but they had to restrain her partner. It seemed like all hell broke loose, he was just livid. He carried on until they had to call the police. They sent two detectives around to investigate and they ended up taking her away in handcuffs. Like on '*Dragnet*'.

That broke up the game for that night, but I don't know how it turned out because I never went back there.

Like I said: "*You can learn a lot from the Old Masters.*"

"Of Course I Play This Game."

I just love partners who seem to 'know' all of the rules, but can't follow any of them. In fact, the only time they go down is when they've taken you out of your bid.

As I have been heard to note often, sometimes my partner seems to be my own worst enemy. (Whoever said that Pinochle doesn't have a 'dummy' hand?)

When Defenders Should Push Trumps

Here's a hand where East used the Barricade bid. South was glad of not persisting to 70. East however, was only trying to push the bidding up, never expecting to be left at 65.

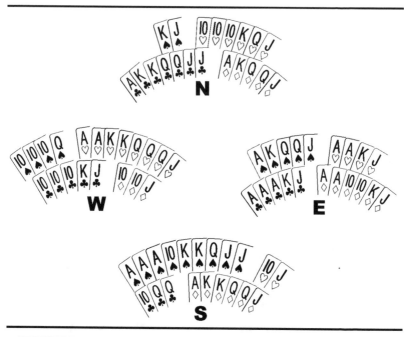

SOUTH	WEST	NORTH	EAST
50	Pass	52	65
Pass		Pass	Spades

South feels better finding that Spades are trump. East needs 27 for the bid and South has his eyes on a bete [set].

East leads off with double *Ace of Diamonds* and then follows with a *Jack of Diamonds*.

South could have let it go around to his partner but chose to step up and push the trump. He knows East does not have the ten, since he melded ace, king, queen and jack, but not a run. So, if his intent is to stop West from ruffing diamonds, he should play the triple *Ace of Spades* and another spade to clear the suit. He knows the *Ten* will push East's *Ace* out, wherever it is, and if he picks up the three *Tens*, his *King of Spades* will bring the *Ace* down.

Instead South leads the *Queen of Spades* {?} topped by West's *Ten* and East's *Ace*. East then leads the *King of Diamonds* to let West trump with a *Ten*. West returns the *King of Hearts* to East's *Ace*. Another diamond lead is trumped by West, this time with the *Queen of Spades*.

The *King of Hearts* is returned to East's *Ace* again. This time East cashes the triple *Ace of Clubs* before returning his last diamond. West trumps with the last *Ten of Trumps*, North's *King of Trumps* [♠] falling helplessly under the steam roller.

North/South have all the rest for 21 HCP total, but what in the world happened? They should pull no less than 31 HCP!

Look at how things should have been done with all of the power that South holds in his hand.

If South plays triple *Ace of Spades* and another, West's *Ten* forces out the *Ace* and it's a different ball game! South has **NINE Spades**, and should lose only **one of them**, the *Ace*.

Defenders need to learn when to lead their trumps early, instead of saving them for the end. Until that time, the prosecution will always beat the defense!

Pick Up Extra Counters with Aces

Defenders must constantly use chances to increase their HCPs. Two counters on one trick are good, three are better and four are Great! The melds are shown for all four players.

You are sitting South and observe the following bidding with East/West taking the hand melding 45 points. This means that they need 25 HCP to keep from being set.

SOUTH	WEST	NORTH	EAST
52	Pass	Pass	60
Pass	65	Pass	70
	Pass		Hearts

Now let's look at your whole hand:

A A K Q J   A K Q J   10 10 K Q Q J   A A Q J J
♠ ♠ ♠ ♠ ♠   ♥ ♥ ♥ ♥   ♣ ♣ ♣ ♣ ♣ ♣   ♦ ♦ ♦ ♦ ♦

East's opening lead is the *Ace of Spades* with West pitching the *King of Spades*, next is the *Ace of Diamonds*, West contributing the *Ten*. East's third lead is the *Queen of Hearts*. You now have as much information about the hand as you need for a successful defense.

You know that East has no winners in clubs because he has shown aces in the three other suits. You most certainly can reach your partner in spades and diamonds because you two have the only aces left in the suits. Two problems possibly confront you. West may have double *Ace of Clubs* and play them first, picking up East's losers. This is very possible since you have six clubs yourself. The second problem could even now be stalking you. West may be able to get in with *Ace of Hearts* immediately. Therefore you must not dally! Step up lively with the *Ace of Hearts* and switch to the *King of Spades*.

Hopefully West has preserved a nice *Ten* for your partner's *Ace*. [That's a 3 point play instead of cashing your *Ace* for just 2 points.] True, he could have avoided giving up that point by giving his partner the *Ten* earlier instead of the *King*, but let's hope he didn't. Your partner seems to be on your wavelength as he lays down double *Ace of Clubs* and a club continuation that runs around to West's *Ace*. West plays the trump ace for unknown reasons, and exits with a spade around to your *Ace*.

Why has West discontinued trumps and switched to spades? Can't be short in spades and wanting to trump a losing spade. We know that not to be the case, because West melded four spades, and gave up a *Ten* to us. So all your aces are safe from ruffing by Responder and all you have to do is keep East ruffing the clubs. Watch for the three point plays.

Here is the full hand to review:

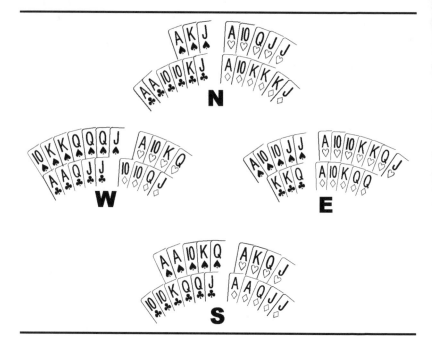

Here are the killer leads that picked up extra counters:

South / *King of Spades* → South / *Queen of Diamonds*
North / *King of Spades* → North / *King of Diamonds*

These leads must often be made <u>Before</u> playing your aces. If Declarer has only two cards in a side suit, he will be trumping the third round. So if you play off your double *Ace* you get 4 points on the two tricks, 2 for your aces and 2 for your partners counters.

However, if you start out with a *King* and RHO is forced to contribute a point on the first trick, then partner comes back with a counter, you have made 5 points on the same two tricks. Don't sniff at the extra point! Pinochle is a game of INCHES.

If you pinch your Inches, the Miles will bring smiles. Remember on the opening *Ace of Spades* lead, West pitched the *King* leaving himself vulnerable with the *Ten*. Suppose partner was trumping the third round. Playing the *Ten* first, avoids being forced to play it on the opponent's trick.

Know When To Hold 'Em

Kenny Rogers said, "*You've got to know when to hold em, and know when to fold em*". That applies to your aces also, as you can see when you follow the play of this hand.

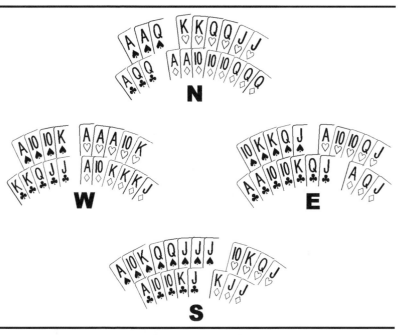

SOUTH	WEST	NORTH	EAST
51	52	53	60
65	Pass	Pass	70
75			Spades

West was humming that song for a few days after this hand was played. North's free bid of 53 showed some power values. So South's only fear on this hand was letting the defenders save, giving them 50 points on this hand.

The opening lead of *Jack of Diamonds* is unorthodox, since it exposes Declarer's short suit. However, it starts rumblings in West's head. South has already shown three diamonds in the meld and now it appears South is attempting to let North start ruffing them. West rises with the *Diamond Ace* and pushes the *Ten of Trump* [♠] which puts North in with the *Ace*. South wisely only contributes a *Jack*.

North recognizes the chance to establish the diamond suit while still holding a stopper in clubs. That stalwart soul accordingly plays double *Ace of Diamonds* catching East's *Ace* and continues diamonds. East trumps in with *Queen of Spades*, South overtrumps with the *King* then leads *Queen of Spades*. West tries to run the *Ten*, which is caught by North's *Ace*. North's *Queen of Spades* return asks *South* to clear the trump suit. So South plays the *Ace of Spades* and knocks out West's last trump stopper by playing the *Jack of Spades* to West's *Ace*.

Instead of looking elsewhere for tricks or knocking out North's club stopper, West blandly continues diamonds to let South trump. South trumps the diamond, plays *Ace of Clubs* and the last two trumps, so North can pitch losing hearts. When South now crosses to North's *Ace of Clubs*, North cashes three more diamonds and lets East/West take the last four tricks with *Ace of Hearts* and three winning clubs for only 14 HCP.

What about West's three *Aces of Hearts*? Still holding them. Oops! Now folding them.

CHAPTER 13 - INSIDE THE MIND

"Partner, Don't sit there with a long face and keep passing.
Bid Something, even if you have Nothing.
At least I'll know you're still in the game!"

Did you ever wish that you could look into the heads of the players and know why they played a particular card? This is what they're thinking as it happens. Is this hand familiar?

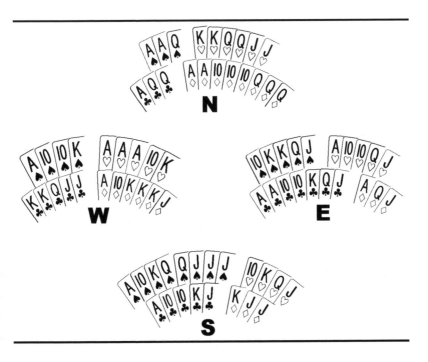

WEST	NORTH	EAST	SOUTH
51	Pass	60	65
Pass		70	80
		Pass	Spades

Follow the players reasoning during the play[21].

South: "THANKS PARTNER, THOSE TEN POINTS WERE ALL I NEEDED."

North: "NO PROBLEM, THAT'S WHY I'M HERE."

What on Earth were They Thinking?

South ponders: *'I hope my partner can pick up a couple of my losers. Let's see if I can get over there with the trump suit.'* Leads *Queen of Spades.*

West: *'South is trying to slide by me with a trump. I know that I can probably turn a few hearts because South showed three and North melded four so I don't have to worry about them getting trumped. My longest suit is diamonds and South is probably short in them so I would like to get our top diamonds in first. Let me get in right away and play my diamonds.'* Plays *Ace of Spades* and *Ace of Diamonds.*

Partner East follows with the *King of Spades* and *Queen of Diamonds (*not the *Jack*, which encourages a continuation).

West thinks: *'How can I get over to my partner now? I know I have to lose a heart anyway so I'll take a chance that my partner can turn a heart. I don't want South or North to be able*

---

[21]In the following dialogue, and later examples, *Mixed Case (in Italics)* sentences indicate player's thinking; while those shown in ALL CAPS signify actual conversation.

to turn the ten and ace, so I better make sure they can only turn the ace, if they have it.' Leads *Ten of Hearts* taken by East.

East observes: '*Well, my partner reached me. I was hoping another diamond was not played.*' Leads *Ace of Diamonds*, and double *Ace of Clubs*, returns *King of Clubs*.

South wonders: '*What's going on here? Someone is going to trump these clubs soon, I'd better try to stop this suit now if its not too late already.*' Plays *Ace of Clubs*, catching partner's *Ace*. Now decides '*Oh, that's the deal. Then I may as well let partner trump these clubs while she still has trumps.*'

[Oops, bad choice, should have tried to get the trump out of the way by leading it.] South now leads *Ten of Clubs,* trumped by North's *Ace of Spades.*

North then waffles: '*I hate to use my ace like this, let me try to get in a diamond or two,*' plays *Ten of Diamonds*. Leads another *Ten of Diamonds*, trumped by East's *King of Spades* and South's *Ten*.

South then continues: "*Maybe partner can trump another club.*" Leads last *Ten of Clubs* trumped by North's *Ace of Spades*.

North worries: '*I don't want to make my partner trump again, I better push the hearts since partner showed three in the meld.*' Plays *Queen of Hearts* taken by West's *Ace*.

Below is the situation after the twelfth trick:

N

W

E

S

West now reasons: '*I know my partner has more clubs, maybe there's a way to get partner leading again.*' Leads *King of Hearts* to East's *Ten.*

East gasps: '*Whoa, how did that happen? Partner wants me in for some reason. All I've got left are spades and clubs, I guess partner wants clubs led.*' Leads *Ten of Clubs* trumped by South's *King of Spades* and West's *Ten.*

South mutters under his breath: "Grrrr!!"

West reasons: '*Nice trick! Let's try another diamond.*' Leads king trumped by East's *Queen of Spades* and South's *Ace.*

South impetuously reasons: '*Let them get this heart and maybe a big trump will fall.*' Leads *Ten of Hearts*. [Faulty reasoning! A more likely distribution for hearts was 6-5-5-4. So it's against the odds to hope for a high trump to jump onto this trick. Lead of a small spade would pull two for one, preventing them from turning their trump separately.]

West pounces: '*Yes! That makes our 20 HCP. I wonder if partner has any more spades?*' Leads *Ten of Diamonds* trumped by East's *Ten of Spades*, South under-ruffing.

Now it is North's turn to mutter: "Arrrgh!!"

East observes: '*Let's try the club thing again, and see what happens.*' Leads *Ten of Clubs* ruffed by South with the *Jack of Spades* and over-ruffed by West's *King of Spades*.

West then deduces: '*If I give up the heart I can make Bonus for last trick.*' Leads *Ace of Hearts* trumped by South.

South moans inwardly: '*I can't believe what just happened. I don't think I made it!*' Leads *Queen of Spades*, which West wins for 32 HCP.

West intones proudly: "GOOD JOB PARTNER!"

East responds, doubly so: "YOU TOO PARTNER, I THINK WE JUST SET THEM!"

South mumbles incoherently: "SORRY PARTNER."

North responds: "GOOD TRY, PARTNER". Then muttering to himself: '*I can't believe he played this hand so badly! Crudbuckets! What was he thinking?*'

Prepare to Change Strategies

Lets listen in again on the reasoning of the players as we follow this next hand.

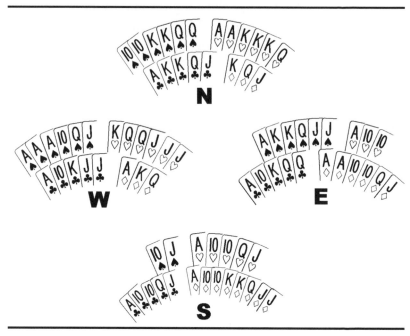

SOUTH	WEST	NORTH	EAST
50	Pass	53	Pass
54		Pass	
Diamonds			

Now let's follow the play of the cards.

South: '*Hmm, partner had exactly 30 points, I hope she has at least three aces, maybe we can pull this off if we can get the top trumps out of the way.*' Plays *Queen of Diamonds*.

West notes observantly: '*I know partner has aces, how many I don't know, but I'd like to get the lead over to him as soon as possible.*' Plays *King of Diamonds* won by East's *Ten*.

East considers his options: '*I have seven tricks and four potential stoppers in trump with this lead. I need to get my longest suit started in hopes that Declarer will be trumping it. I have six spades and my RHO showed four spades in the meld so I'll try spades.*' Plays *Ace of Hearts*, partner plays *Ace* on *Ace*. Plays *Ace of Spades* and *King of Spades* next.

West wins with *Ace* and considers: '*So my partner thinks we should push spades, I was undecided between hearts and spades. Now I know for sure.*' Continues with *Ten of Spades*.

South bemoans: '*Lucky stiffs, found out my weakness quickly.*' Trumps with *King of Diamonds* and leads *Jack* [♦].

West immediately assesses things: '*No need to delay with this ace any longer, our mission is clear.*' Takes *Ace of Diamonds*, plays *Jack of Spades*.

South worries: '*East is all over me with what looks like double ace. I've got to get my partner in to lead trump through him.*' Trumps with *King of Diamonds* and leads *Ten of Hearts*.

North assumes: '*Maybe I can help my partner with a trump lead.*' Takes trick with *Ace of Hearts* and leads *King of Trumps* [♦].

East reasons: '*I'll stop this lead with an ace and I'll still control the trump suit with Ace, Ten, Queen.*' Plays *Ace of Diamonds* and returns *Jack of Spades*.

South can only hope: '*I need to change my strategy and get East to ruff something.*' Ruffs with *Ten*, leads *Ace of Hearts* and then the *Ten*.

East sums things up quickly: '*He only has two trump left. I'll make him play his last one.*' Trumps with the *Ten*, plays *Ace of Diamonds*, partner pitches *Ace of Spades*. East then leads *Queen of Spades*.

South trumps with *Ace of Diamonds*. Leads *Queen of Clubs* to North's *Ace of Clubs*.

North returns *Queen of Clubs*, taken by West. Club return taken by East.

East plays *Ace of Clubs* and club return won by South. Last trick won by East with trump.

North/South takes 23 HCP.

Here you had a chance to observe the thought processes which drive the play of the hand. To really play this game well, you need to figure out why each player is doing what they do. Then you can either defend against it, or take advantage of it. As you see, it involves a constant shifting and re-evaluation as more pieces are added to the puzzle. You have to be prepared to change strategy as the other players make their moves to either complement or thwart your original plan. If you just follow the cards on the table, well, anybody can do that.

Now do you see what is so fascinating about this game?

Where to Play Aces for the Most Payback

Do you play Aces In Places, [AIP] or Aces On Spaces? [AOS] In Places, means places where they can pick up 2, 3, and 4 points. In Spaces, is where they pull only 1 or 2 points. Watch to see how aces can be used to carry a full load of points.

East showed remarkable restraint in not pushing for the bid on this hand,. Very few players holding a six-card suit, 50 meld and six aces to boot, would allow the opponents to buy a hand for 65. Most would even call it Cowardly! Especially opposite a partner who opened with an aces bid.

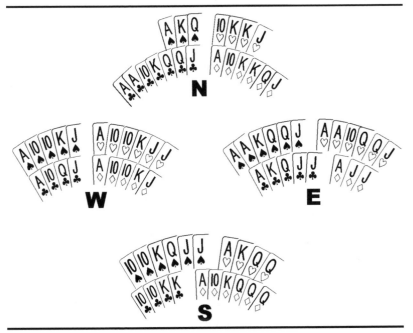

WEST	NORTH	EAST	SOUTH
51	53	60	65
Pass	Pass	Pass??	Diamonds

Whatever the reason, South gets the bid in diamonds and is rewarded with a run by partner. With a total of 58 Meld and matching runs, it seems like a walkover. But don't be too sure. North/South still need 20 HCP to save this one.

#	North	East	South	West
1	A♦	J♦	►Q♦	K♦{!}
2	►A♠	J♠	K♠	J♠
3	►Q♠	K♠{!}	10♠	A♠
North. {?} Trying to get a cut.				
4	J♦	A♦	Q♦	►10♦
West. {!} Eliminating trumps from the game.				
5	Q♦	►J♦	Q♦	10♦
6	K♦	10♥	K♦	►A♦
7	K♦	J♥	10♦	►J♦
8	K♠	A♠	►J♠	K♠
9	K♥	Q♥ {!}	A♥	►J♥
10	10♦	Q♠	►10♠	10♠
South. {?} What's the rush to cut the ten of spades?				
11	►Q♣	A♣	K♣	10♣
North. Finally trying to get his clubs set up.				
12	J♥	►A♥	Q♥	K♥
13	K♥	►A♥	Q♥	10♥
East. Get out of partner's way with heart stoppers.				
14	10♥	►Q♥	K♥	10♥
15	K♣	J♣	A♦	►J♥
16	J♣	K♣	►10♣	A♣
17	Q♣	J♣	J♠	►A♥
East. Pitches worthless club, waiting for spade.				
18	10♣	A♠	Q♠	►10♠
19	A♣	►Q♠	K♣	J♣
20	A♣	►Q♠	10♣	Q♣

North/South were set with only 17 HCP. How could that happen? Rather, how did East/West **cause** that to happen?

Note *Trick 1*, West refuses to play Aces On Spaces. (AOS) *Trick 3*, East refuses AOS to allow partner to unblock suit. Also, *Trick 7,* West refuses AOS to get trump out.

Later, *Trick 9*; East refuses AOS to remove South's stopper in heart first. Finally, at *Trick 11*, East has good timing in taking the *Ace of Clubs*, clearing hearts while partner retained the club stopper.

Naturally, on Monday morning it's easy to see the quarterback's mistake at the end of the first half. [*Trick 10*] Also, to see that North could have tried to set up the clubs earlier. South knew the only hope was in North's having club values. Since North can always cut the spade, a better play would be the *Ten of Clubs* by South at **Trick 8..**

This knocks out West's club stopper before the hearts are cleared. If the clubs are set up first, North can run the suit when eventually getting the spade ruff.

The key to the killing defense on this hand was the refusal by East / West to play aces on empty 'Spaces'.

Their aces were carefully preserved for 'Places' where points were available.

CHAPTER 14 - PSYCHOLOGICAL WARFARE

Master Player: Plays while eating a club sandwich and hot fudge sundae without messing up the cards.

It's all well and good to say you're just playing for the fun of the game, and winning is not the only thing that matters. The fact remains that competition is the spice of the game. If no competition exists, there's really no point to keeping score. Just bid and play. Getting set means nothing and making the bid means even less.

Getting back to planet Earth now, we find humans down there. They have a need to excel, to do better, to push the envelope, yes to compete! Our society's structure is based on getting ahead. Nowhere in our social order do you find Losers glorified. While we accept losing as a necessary evil, we expect our team to win. So let us now devote a portion of our discussion to the human factors that generate our rivalry and stir our emotions to the feverish pitch of, dare we say it? Competition! No need for us to stir up competition. It's There!

Human Factors, that's the key! We must learn to isolate and recognize the human factors in our game. The first humans to consider are ourselves. Each of us has a certain tolerance level for pain and stress that we must acknowledge for our well-being. If this level is constantly infringed upon, we become irritable, lose our enjoyment (and ability to think.) There are no arbitrary rules to govern these built-in parameters. They are a given, for each of us. We must learn to concede our limitations and work within them. Some of us enjoy living on the brink. Others over the years develop a conservative bent that precludes taking unnecessary chances. Unfortunately in pinochle, this affects one's bidding and play of the hand.

Recognizing these tendencies in ourselves, helps us to take advantage of the same factors when dealing with others. I'm sure you know players who just will not give up a bid. They would rather take a bid for 70 and go down by 2 or 3 points than to give it to the opponents for 65. Whereas other players never bid up to the full potential of their hands. How do you deal with this? In short, Play the Players! Against stronger players, you may play more conservatively due to their superior defensive skills. With players who are ace slingers, we tend to bid a little more recklessly, feeling we may get help in making our bid.

By the same token, you must know how others view you, regardless of how you personally feel about your game. If you are viewed as a professional, that tends to engender respect for your bids and the defense you are expected to muster up. This is an edge for you! Not enough can be said about the value of a positive outlook when playing Pinochle.

Good Players Don't Need to use Putdowns

Advanced players seldom need to use degrading ploys in accomplishing their objectives. They have no need to denigrate the opponent's skills and accomplishments, or berate their partners for real or imagined shortcomings. These tactics can only serve to diminish the joy of the game and tarnish whatever reputation you may possess. Rather than make you look better, it reduces your partner's confidence in your ability, which can only benefit the opponents.

A kind word to the opponents after a hand, not only enhances your expert appeal, but may even lull the opposition into a false sense of security or carelessness which might permit you to escape unscathed from a potential upset.

Keep an Eye on the Scoresheet

Learn to play according to the score. Of course it is best if possible, to get off to an early lead, as that will affect the tone of the game. Players tend to bid more aggressively when they are behind. So when you are in the lead, you may in fact bid stronger, since the losers will often bid higher to catch up, then let them have it! When you are leading by a large margin, avoid taking needless chances on borderline hands, other than for pushing the opponents up. However, when you are behind by a significant amount, that is the time to push the envelope on hands that present any probability of a make. When contending for contracts, remember that a distributional hand often wins out when competing against strong hands that are flat and even.

As a result, don't be afraid to stick your neck out and take a chance, but by the same token don't get a reputation as an over-bidder. Good players will not only be able to read you more easily, but another undesirable side effect accrues. Your partners begin to slant their bidding in an effort to accommodate your known tendencies. Now, you have no way of knowing whether their meld bids are true or if they are holding back to make up for your boisterous bidding.

If boldness happens to be your strength, do not let it become your weakness. Try to keep your game face consistent, so that it's unreadable as far as possible. It should not be readily apparent when you are out on a limb.

When you are flush, let the world be surprised. Learn to assess the strengths and foibles of others, then try to play just beyond the margins those limitations suggest.

Thanks for the Memories

Often I'm asked what was my most memorable hand. That's a pretty tall order considering how many years I'd have to cull through. There are two or three however, that stand out.

One hand I remember from the late 80's was at a late night session in Queens, NYC at Thomas' home. We were playing against him, and his son Terry and leading them by 439 to 169. Two other players were waiting for the losers to get up. All we needed was a bid to go out. I dealt and picked up my hand last, which looked something like this:

My RHO bid 50, my partner passed and Terry said: "***Well, no need to fool around with this hand, I bid 100.***" I said to myself, '*he picked up one good hand, probably double aces or a double run. I'll just boost him a little,*' so I bid 110. As long as I live I'll never forget his next words. He said: "***OK, you got it.***" I said: "***What?***" He said: "***You got it for 110.***"

Well, you could have poured me through a crack in the table, I was that watery. As I threw the hand in, my partner stared at me in amazement. "*I had 9 aces*" he whispered hoarsely. Terry said: "***I had nothing, and nothing to lose, you were winning the game anyway.***" We went back 110 points and they went on to win the game. I never forgot that hand.

It also taught me that there's a little Poker in Pinochle. After all, Pinochle is not just about cards. Anybody can get good cards. Mainly, it's about people. Learn how they differ, how to read them, and structure your game accordingly.

Perhaps the most powerful testimony to the humanity of this game comes from a V. A. Hospital where I was privileged to lecture.

One player there had survived a land mine incident. As a result, he sustained the loss of both hands and a substantial portion of his face and neck including one eye.

He remains an avid Pinochle player. On occasion, there is no one available to set up his hand and turn the cards for him. As a result, he designed and had built a cardholder with round wire prongs numbered on both sides from one through twenty.

After his cards were dealt, one of the players would slip each of his cards face down into one of the prongs. The holder is then flipped around facing him to survey the hand from this kaleidoscope viewpoint.

During the melding period, he calls out the appropriate numbers and the player closest pulls those cards for him. During play of the hand, the same occurs.

His disposition is warm and cordial with never a hint of discontent or complaint. All the patients and staff love to play with him and are more than willing to expend themselves in his behalf.

PART 5 - VARIATIONS ON THE GAME

CHAPTER 15 - THREE HANDED double-deck PINOCHLE

"Pinochle is not the only game in the world, there may be worlds where there is no Pinochle. But I seriously doubt it!"

Tradition has it that two couples, farmers in the Mid-West, played Pinochle six nights a week for many years. When one member of the set passed away, they had no desire to teach anyone else the game, but were unwilling to give up their nightly pastime. Thus was born Three-Handed Pinochle, with a Widow, or kitty.

Even More Cards

The version of Three-handed that we recommend has most of the features of Four-handed except that each player receives 25 cards. What happens to the other five cards? They are dealt face down as a Widow or Kitty to be awarded to the highest bidder. The bidding starts at 50 and may proceed at one-point intervals to 60, then by 5's. The highest bidder names a trump and must lay down at least a marriage in the trump suit.

The Widow is then exposed for all to view. The 5 cards are taken into the hand of the bidder who then lays down the meld cards and puts away five cards into the Widow which now becomes the bidder's first trick. Obviously this is a good place to *"hide away"* points that otherwise might be given away.

He then picks up the meld off the table and returns it to his hand. Thus, he is not allowed to put any of the melded cards into the kitty.

After bidder's meld is completed, either of the other two players may meld 20 or more, with the proviso that they must bring back at least 15 HCP to retain their meld. (*Bidder must still make 20 HCP as normal.*) If the others choose not to meld, they still get credit for any HCP made. The bidder starts off the play as usual and all covering rules apply.

During hand play, the game changes significantly. The defenders on each hand combine their forces in an attempt to set the bidder. If truth be told, it is much easier to defend than play against two experienced defenders. Many a bidder has melded cards putting them well over their bid only to find they cannot make the required 20 HCP.

The usual policy is for the two players with lower scores to pool their resources to defeat the player with the higher score. As long as one of the defenders does not get greedy, this works.

But check out the following scenario. Player A has no score. The bid is dropped on him for 50. P. At this point Player B, a better player, melds 90 and must make 15 points to save.

Player C may choose to help Player A instead of giving his points to Player B because he would rather not have the better player in the lead. If however, Player B had not melded points, then 'C' might choose to help him set 'A' in order to even out the scores. This is why the Three-Handed game is called "*Cut-Throat*".

Most successful three-handed players rely on the Kitty for help but have their limits as to how much to expect.

Let's Try a Round

Here are three sample hands from a three-handed game.

[Note: Remember, there will be 25 cards in your hand now. And you were complaining about holding just 20 before.]

Player #1 - Louis:

Louis' hand has 39 meld with hearts as trump. Adding on 20 HCP will bring him to 60. What can he reasonably expect from the kitty? *King of Diamonds* would bring his meld to 49. *Ace of Diamonds* would bring it to 129.

What are the chances that of three *Diamond Aces* available, one will be in the Widow? Realistically, his Safe Bid is 60. His Normal Bid would be 70. His Risk Bid as well as his Wild Bid would be 150, counting on finding the *Ace of Diamonds* in the Kitty.

Player #2 - Jake:

Jake's hand contains 45 meld in support of hearts or spades. However, he would meld the same no matter who took the bid. So what would be the point of risking a set when he would more likely make 15 HCP as a defender than 20 HCP as the Declarer.

Therefore, he should make the Safe Bid of 65, with no Risk Bid. Especially holding only four aces out of 16.

Player #3 - Lydia:

Lydia's hand contains 63 in meld with clubs or diamonds as trump. Her Safe Bid is 85. She has no reason to Risk Bid as she has very little to gain from the Widow.

This is perforce, the Widow (or Kitty). Who would it have helped?

Lydia takes the bid for 75 in diamonds. She shows a 15 point run, double pinochle, aces, queens and jacks for 65 meld. She places the *Ten of Hearts* along with double *Ten* and double *Jack of Spades* in the widow for a 3 point start.

Observing the *Diamond King* on her right, she leads the *Queen of Diamonds* taken by Jake, with the *Ace*. *Ace of Hearts* and the *Queen of Hearts* puts Lydia back in with the *Ace*. Lydia plays *Jack of Diamonds* taken by Jake with the *King*. Return is another *Queen of Hearts* won by Louis. *Ace of Hearts* is led and the next *Ace* is trumped by Lydia's *King of Diamonds*.

King of Clubs goes to Jake's *Ace*. *Queen of Hearts* return trumped by Lydia with the *King of Diamonds*. *King of Clubs* is taken by Louis with the *Ace*.

Lydia trumps another heart with the *Ten of Diamonds* and leads back the *Club Ten* taken by Louis' *Ace*.

Ten of Hearts trumped by Jake's Ten and Lydia's *Ace*.

Lydia now cashes the Ten and *Ace of Clubs* and exits with a club trumped by Jake with the *Jack*. Jake leads back the *Queen of Spades* taken by Lydia's *Ace*.

Lydia's *Club Queen* trumped by Jake's *Queen of Diamonds,* next leads *King of Spades* to Louis' *Spade Ace*. Louis leads another *Spade Ace* then Lydia trumps the next spade with the *Ten* and exits with the last club.

Queen of Club return taken by Louis' *Ten of* Diamonds, who then pushes the *Jack of Diamonds to dislodge Lydia's Ace.* Last trick is Louis' with the trump *Ace*.

Queen of Spades return forces Lydia's *Ace* for her last trick.

The Bidder Lydia, #3 makes her bid with 20 HCP.

Jake, #2 fails to save meld with only 9 HCP.

Louis, #1 holds his own with 43 meld and 19 HCP on this hand.

Perhaps not a game you want to make a career of, but it does serve as a filler while waiting for a fourth to show up.

Funny thing, I've found that once you get started in a three-handed game, the fourth player does show up, just when the game gets interesting.

Not so Great for Couples

I used to play three-handed with a bachelor friend when we worked together. He got married recently, surprising me, considering that he was 55 years old. I understand that the guests at the wedding were on pins and needles waiting well past the appointed time of 3:00 PM.

The bride was in fact early, but the groom and his party had not been heard from, leading some to believe that he had gotten cold feet (*pre-wedding jitters.*)

Relief was evident when the groomsmen made their appearance from the vestry behind the altar and the rites were commenced shortly after 3:45.

Later that night, after the guests had left and the loving couple were ensconced in the honeymoon suite, the bride made known her earlier misgivings at her husbands late arrival, At this the groom protested that he was not really late.

When asked why his party took so long to come into the church, he admitted that they were actually in the ministers study, but did not want to stop in the middle of the Pinochle game which took longer than he had expected.

Since the suite had no couch, one wonders if he spent that first night in the bathtub?

"Forgot the Kitty Again!"

CHAPTER 16 - TWO HANDED double-deck PINOCHLE
"Practice does not make Perfect, but if you don't practice, you will not even make as far as Good."

Here is an entertaining game for two players. It highlights math skills to figure the odds of cards in the Kitty.

As in three-handed both players get 25 cards. This version of the game combines the attraction of a five-card kitty and a third hand of 25 cards which lies 'dead' until taken by the winner of the last trick. The kitty goes to the highest bidder, but the third hand goes to the taker of the last trick. So if you expect to make your bid, you'd better plan on getting the last trick.

If your opponent finds your short suit early by playing one of their long suits, your trumps can go up in smoke very quickly. The real skill is in knowing how to throw away. You must throw away the suit that the defender is short in and keep as many as possible in the suit that he is long in.

How do you know which is which? That comes with experience. I know one young man to whom I spoon fed this game, that I cannot beat at it now. The aggravating thing is, I don't know why! He consistently outguesses me.

Declarer still needs 20 HCP to save, and defender must make at least 15 HCP to save meld. The odds for getting the card you want are the same as in three-handed because there are still 55 cards that you have no clue as to their location.

All the principles of Safe bidding, Normal bidding, Risk bidding, and Wild bidding apply here. Also Bluff bidding to keep one out of the Kitty, or simply just to Bid Em Up Higher!

Bidding Out to Win the Game

Many players have the requirement, that a team must bid out rather than meld out. This prevents one from just sitting on their hands and sliding into glory. You must actually take the bid, which moves you over 500, in order to win the game. Others play it differently, so that anytime you reach 500, you win, regardless of whether you took the bid or not.

If this rule is played, the side first reaching the set game amount wins. Some circles allow "declaring out." A player may at any time claim that his side has reached the game number. Play stops and the tricks are examined. If the claim is found to be correct, the claiming side wins, even if the other should have a higher score. If the claim is incorrect, the other side wins at once by default. Of course, if both sides reach or exceed the game amount at the end of a deal, the bidder's side wins.

We would recommend one proviso to place into your two-handed game. When one player's plus score added to the other player's minus score reaches above 500, start a new game. Or, that when one player is past 500 and the other player goes at least 100 minus, the game is over. Otherwise, you could be there all night, on just the one game!

CHAPTER 17 - DUPLICATE double-deck PINOCHLE
"I know he's my partner, who says he ain't heavy?"

"What is this? First single deck, then double-deck, now Duplicate double-deck? I can't do it, no way can I hold that many cards!" All Right Already! Stop with the crying! You don't get more cards. Duplicate just means that everybody gets to play the <u>Same</u> cards! How's that you say? Well, Duplicate double-deck is played with two or more tables of players.

At each table the hands are duplicated so everyone gets to play the same hands. At the end of the session scores are compared and the players getting the highest scores on those identical hands, end up as the winners. What happens is that much of the element of chance is taken out of the game. Scores are based not on how good your cards were, but on how much you scored with the hands you were dealt.

Why Everyone Plays the Same Hands

Duplicate Pinochle is suggested by Ram as a result of training in the Bridge world where Duplicate is commonplace. It tends to level the field so that a player catching an unusual run of good cards cannot win all the games. The element of chance is negated by the prior replication of hands to be played. How does this happen?

First, a Director is needed to coordinate the event. The Director may be Playing or Non-Playing. With at least four tables in play, it is recommended that a Non-Playing Director be used. Players must use Duplicate Boards, or Hand-Holders that are prepared in advance.

The hands are shuffled and dealt, then duplicated according to how many tables will be in play. The numbered hands, which are identical, are then put into marked holders and distributed to the corresponding tables of players. A numbered score sheet is included with each dealt hand so that the scores can be entered by each table and tabulated by the Director at the end of the session.

Scores may be compared in several ways according to the number of players present. A Compass Scoring System may be used where four tables or less are in play. Compass, as the name implies, indicates that each pair has played every hand from all sides of the compass, North/South and East/West. Players rotate to play different teams during parts of the session.

Using this system, each partnership plays both sides of the same hand at alternate times during the session. In this way a hand which you played as North/South early in the session, will be played by you as East/West later on during the same session. This gives you the opportunity to better the score made by those who played the same hand.

Now scores are compared twice, once when you play the hand as North/South, and again when you play it as East/West. Since all player's scores are tabulated collectively, only one winning pair emerges from the Compass Scoring System.

Double Top Scoring is used with four tables in play. Here there are two winners each session because you compete or compare scores, only with the players who sit in your same direction. Pairs play each hand only once and the score is cumulative only for those players sitting in the same direction.

Say for the record, that ten hands are being played at five different tables. You, sitting North/South would have your score compared with the results of all other North/South players. If your score was higher than the four other North/South players on five of the hands, you would get a score of 20 on those five hands because you beat four players five times. If you tied with two other pairs on two of the hands, you get a ½ point for the tie scores and zero for the hands in which you were outscored. Likewise the East/West pairs compete with the other pairs sitting in the same direction.

When an even number of pairs are playing in an event, the Team Scoring System may be used. In this variation each North/South partnership is paired with one of the East/West pairs as a team. Scores are compared when both sides of the team play a hand at different tables.

For example, Pair #1 North/South plays Hand A. at Table #1. North/South #1 take the bid and score a total of 73 on the hand. East/West #1 at the same table save their meld for 47 points. At table #2, East/West #2 are in partnership with North/South #1 and North/South #2 are partners with East/West #1. When Table #2 plays Hand A. North/South #2 takes the bid in a different suit and scores only 65 on the hand. However East/West #2 do not save their meld. The team of North/South #1 and East/West #2 score a total of 73 on the hand. The team of North/South #2 and East/West #1 score 65 plus 47 on the same hand, for a difference of 39 points.

The director announces beforehand whether the scoring will be decided by Board-A-Match, where only the total hands won are considered, or if the scores will be converted to Match Points, in which case a table is used to determine the percentage of scores allowed to be counted.

Consider the far-reaching implications of this approach. Since the hand records can be prepared in advance of the tournament, distribution can be made to a larger geographical area. Thus, clubs in different sections of the country, or world can compete simultaneously. With local winners, as well as sectional or regional winners, what a diverse pattern of expertise and culture can be interwoven. Then we will experience the multi-national nature of our game, and benefit from association with Pinochle fans around the world.

I believe that colleges offer the most dynamic future thrust to our game, and that the development of this venue will help to revitalize tired blood in our present systems. Youth has the tendency to innovate and experiment without dependence on staid and moribund standards. I intend to develop seminars and push for education at this level. I challenge these energetic youths to accept the gauntlet of competition in the mentally stimulating environment of International Pinochle.

CHAPTER 18 - PLAYING ON THE INTERNET
"Respect the fact that we are all very different."

There was a time, if you wanted to get up a game of double-deck; you had to really hustle, make a bunch of phone calls, set and re-set times to fit all the possible players.

The entire hassle is now reduced, thanks to the Internet. You can log on[22] and find a game around the clock any day of the week. And they're on-line all the time. The categories are neat also.

You can play in the Social Lounge, where much of the time is spent talking and the game is incidental. You might say it's like a Pinochle Chat Room. There's the Intermediate Lounge, where not too much choice is afforded because very few want to be classified as in between. So what you'll find here are mainly neophytes. And of course there's the Advanced Lounge, where all the specialists are supposed to be.

Just a few words of caution before you get your hopes up for a professional game. There's really no accurate way to rate an expert on the Internet. So just be prepared to suffer with the one you get stuck with.

The rating system is based on the number of games you have played, completed and won. But you won't know if the one you're playing with is a legitimate advanced player or not, because after the game they may change their identity and shed their lost games in favor of a more pleasing persona. Why not kibitz, (look on) a game first?

---

[22]It should be noted that any discussion here about play on the Internet is specific to the Yahoo! Game site.

It's relatively easy to get into the game. You'll need to register and pick a password, give a few vital statistics about yourself and you're in.

Manners

Just pick a Social Room that's not full and enter. As you do, you'll notice many games are in full swing and you may choose to enter one of the rooms and kibitz first. As you enter type in; *"Hello All,"* and ask if it's OK for you to kibitz for a while because you're new. If the host of the table says OK, just click on the 'kibitz' button and watch. Refrain from making any comments about the game or bidding, and when you leave be sure to say *"Thanks all."*

You'll find a host of abbreviations used in the game rooms as the players converse with each other that you may not be familiar with.

Some examples are:

[brb]	Be Right Back
[gga]	Good Game All
[gjp]	Good Job Partner
[gla]	Good Luck All
[gle]	Good Luck Everyone
[gma]	Good Morning All
[lol]	Laughing Out Loud
[nha]	Nice Hand All
[nhb]	Nice Hand Blues
[nhp]	Nice Hand Partner
[nhr]	Nice Hand Reds
[nm]	Nice Meld
[rofl]	Rolling On Floor Laughing
[sp]	Sorry Partner

You might find a warmer welcome in the Intermediate section because hardly anyone in the Advanced section will play with you until you reach a Red rating. This is 1650 points. The Yahoo! game site penalizes advanced players unfairly when novice players beat them.

For example, if you are a novice player and you beat an advanced player, you may pick up 20 to 30 points for the win, the advanced player losing the same amount. However if the advanced player beats you, he may pick up 6 to 8 points, and you only lose the same amount. As a result, advanced players usually only compete with players ranked closest to them, where the won/lost ratio will be equitable.

When you click on the Advanced Lounge, you will see that there are ten different Advanced Lounges, and the number of Players in each at the present time is indicated. You may pick any of them.

Some will indicate [FULL] This means that over 175 Players are in that particular Lounge and entry is now restricted. Should you desire to enter one of the [FULL] Lounges, you may only do so after first logging into Yahoo! You then enter www.shove-it.com which will allow you to enter through the 'back door' of the Lounge.

If you, as a novice or provisional, attempt to sit at a table where advanced players are waiting for a player, you will probably be asked to leave, with the warning: "RED Only Please" or "Too Low." If you ignore this, or attempt to contest it in any way, you will be unceremoniously booted away from the table. At many tables, you will receive no such warning, as soon as you enter, you will be booted out without a word.

Of course you may choose to open your own table as a host, and now you can pick who sits at your table. As a beginner in the game room, you will probably play with anyone willing to sit with you, until you get a Red ranking.

Options

In setting up a table, you will be given several options. One, will be the option to require at least 20 points to score. If you do not check this option, it means that on any hand you play, whatever HCP you score will be credited to your score. The 20 HCP minimum requirement is waived.

Another option is whether your game will be rated or not. Always check this option before the game if you want your results to be recorded.

The next option involves 'Idle Force Forfeiting'. This option enables opponents to win the game by forfeit when you remain idle for over three minutes without playing a card. This option is a source of much misery, often by default. At times you may have trouble with your computer hanging up, or the game server kicks you off. You may find that you cannot get back on-line before the three minutes are up. Meanwhile, the other players can get a sub to replace you until you return, or forfeit you. What happens when you are forfeited? You are first charged with a lost game. Then double the lost points are deducted from your rating. Your partner is credited with a win, and no points are deducted from their score.

You will find that your playing moves are much more proscribed in the game room, since you will be prompted to bid when it is your turn and your meld will be displayed for you as it becomes due, so there is no chance of your missing a meld. Also, the Yahoo! site will not allow you to renege/revoke by playing a wrong card. You are forced by the computer to head up each trick, to follow suit and to trump when void in a suit. Your score is kept for you and a running count of your high card points is maintained. In addition, you are allowed to inspect the last trick played at any time. So you will be held by the hand as it were, more so than in a regular game. But the sad part is that since the players are unknown to each other, there is a tendency to be rude and unkind as they can hide behind their anonymity.

You would therefore be well advised not to offer unsolicited advice to anyone you meet in the game room, for fear you may be roundly vilified or even cursed out for your pains. You may of course hook up with an adequate player who knows the game and defends decently. If so, you might win two or three games before you are accused of having secret signals, talking on a two-way radio or an open phone line. But there is the advantage of always being able to find a game with no more effort than is required to mail a post card.

So if you have a long distance friend who enjoys the game, what better way to spend your leisure, than on the Internet sharpening your skills for the next time you can play face to face. Because face to face really is the only way to truly enjoy the game of Pinochle. That way you get to experience the entire personal interaction engendered by the individual repartee and mingling of close friends who value each other's company.

While you're there on the Internet, don't forget to visit our web site for the latest news from the RAM crew. Happy surfing! ***www.PinochlePress.com***

P.S. By the time you read this, we hope to have our own Game Room set up on our site, where you will be able to enjoy both interactive and computer generated competition.

APPENDICES

GLOSSARY

ACES (AROUND): A unit of Meld in which a player shows at least one ace in each suit, resulting in a credit of 10 to the partnership score. Double Aces credits 100, and Triple Aces, scores 300, by agreement. Most players agree on rules, which require mandatory declaration of aces even if partnerships don't have the minimum 20 Meld between them. For example, you have 12 meld with aces; your partner has 6 meld. With only 18 points you cannot get credit for meld,but you must make the declaration: *"I have aces."* On the Internet this requirement is moot, as all meld is shown whether or not it totals 20.

AROUND: Any Meld combination of Aces or face cards that appears in each of the four suits; Spades, Hearts, Clubs and Diamonds. Also, the combination of a marriage in each suit is commonly known as a ROUNDHOUSE (see below).

AUCTION: A series of bids by players to inform partners of their strength and determine who will name trumps and at what level. E.g. once a player passes, they are unable to re-enter the auction during that hand.

AVERAGE HAND: A hand that contains 10 meld points and four aces is the average expectation of each player before the hands are seen. Therefore the minimum for opening a hand is normally 20 points and four aces with at least a six-card trump suit. This presupposes partner's 10 meld and four aces to allow for the making of at least 50 when the mandatory 20 HCPs are added to the total.

BALANCED HAND: A hand with even distribution, containing no voids, singletons, or doubletons and no more than one tripleton. Hand must also contain no suit longer than six cards in length. (*See also Flat Hand*)

BARE RUN: A trump sequence of five cards with no other cards in the trump suit.

BARRICADE BID: A bid designed to disrupt communications and block out the opponents from finding their best fit.

BETE: Pronounced [bayt] A bidder who goes set, or fails to fulfill a contract is said to be bete. E.g. "We *took the last bid, but on the first hand you went bete for 65.*"

BID: An undertaking to make at least a certain number in meld and high cards combined. E.g. "*I'm sorry, I didn't hear if you made a bid.*"

BID OUT: When game is within reach of a partnership they must take a bid to complete the game rather than melding out. This is called bidding out. (*See also MELDING OUT*)

BID UP: To continue bidding against an opponent without sufficient values to make the bid. Usually done with the object of causing the opponent to go set.

BIDDING: The process by which players contract for the privilege of naming trump, at different levels during an auction.

BLOCKED SUIT: When one partner holds high cards in their hand which prevent the other partner from taking all the winning tricks which they hold.

BOARD: (*See BONUS*)

BOARD SET: Occurs when the bidding team cannot meld at least 20 points. Also, when the bidding team has insufficient meld to bring it within 50 points of the final bid, making it impossible to fulfill the bid under any circumstances. E.g. A team bids 75 and melds 22. Even if their team made all 50 HCP, their total could only be 72, thus they are Board Set.

BONUS: An extra two points added to the high card points of a team scoring the last trick of each hand. E.g. There are 48 HCP in the deck plus a 2-point bonus for last trick.

BOOK: (*See TRICK*)

BOSTON: When a partnership wins all 20 tricks in a given hand, they are said to have run a Boston, or sent the opponents to Boston. This is very rarely done. (*See also TRICKLESS, BURNT, PINOCHLE*)

BREAK: How the missing cards in a suit are divided between the opponents. E.g. when seven cards are missing in the suit, lopsided distribution finds them divided 6-1, a bad break. Whereas a good break discovers them to be 4-3.

BRING BACK: The amount of High Card Points needed to complete a bid or validate one's meld. E.g. *"The bid was 65 and we melded 39, so we had to Bring Back 26."*

BURNED, BURNT: *(See TRICKLESS)*

CALL: Any bid or pass.

CASH: To play a winning card or cards. E.g. *"I don't know why I didn't cash my ace of hearts while I was in Partner, that would have set them."*

CHOKE: To ruff with a higher trump in front of a player who must also ruff. The second player is now choked out; being forced to follow with a smaller trump.

CLAIMING: To lay cards on the table and declare that one has the rest of the tricks without playing the hand out. If the claimer does not state the order in which the cards will be played, an opponent has the right to select any of the shown cards which they can win, and claim that trick or tricks, as their own.

COMBINED HANDS: All the cards in both hands belonging to one partnership.

CONDONE: To forgive an irregularity by an opponent. For example, if the wrong player leads and the next player in turn plays to the trick, the lead out of turn is condoned. No penalty.

CONTRACT: The undertaking by Declarer's side to furnish at least 20 meld, plus 20 or more high card points to fulfill the number of the final bid in the auction. [*Meld alone is not enough. At least 20 points of the contract must be in HCP regardless of the amount of the Meld*]

COUNTER: Any ace, ten or king on a completed trick belonging to a partnership. Counters are each scored as one HCP. E.g. *"We turned one book that had no counter at all on it."* (*See also HONOR CARDS*)

COVER: To play a card higher than that already played on a trick. Also called Heading Up. Pinochle rules call for all players in turn; to cover any previously played cards on a trick. E.g. It is not a violation to ask partner if he has failed to cover a trick, just as you would ask when he fails to follow suit.

CRAWL: (*See COVER*)

CROSS-CUT, CROSS-RUFF: Leading a card from one hand to allow partner to ruff or trump that card and partner then leading back another suit which the other partner is ruffing or trumping. To lead back and forth for the purpose of ruffing.

CUT (SUIT, or LEAD): To play a trump on the lead of a side suit.

CUT (THE CARDS): To divide the deck into two sections and place the bottom portion on top. The RHO normally does the cut.

DEAL: The act of distributing cards to the four players. Dealer passes cards first to the player on his left, then proceeds clockwise until all have received 20 cards. Cards may be distributed in sets of either four or five cards. Not more or less.

DEALER: The player whose turn it is to distribute the cards. Each hand the deal moves clockwise. Player to the left of dealer has first opportunity to bid. Dealer is assumed to have bid 50 if the other three players pass. Thus the expression, *'dropped on the dealer'*. No hands are passed out in Pinochle.

DECLARER: Player bidding highest in the auction who has the privilege of naming the trump suit. Declarer must have a marriage in the suit named, for it to be trump.

DEFEAT: To stop Declarer from making the contract. (*See also BETE and SET*)

DEFENSE: The partnership that did not make the highest bid or win the contract.

DISCARD: To throw off a card from another suit when you are unable to follow suit and can't play a trump. (*See also THROW OFF*)

DISCOURAGING BID: A bid which discourages partner from bidding again.

DISTRIBUTION: The number of cards initially held in each suit by a particular player.

DIX: [*pronounced deece*] The lowest card in a single Pinochle deck, (the Nine). These cards are eliminated from the double Pinochle deck leaving the jack as the lowest ranking card.

DOUBLE ACES: Two aces in each of the four suits, also called a thousand aces.

DOUBLE DUMMY: To play a hand in theory while looking at all four hands. A puzzle that is designed to test ones skill at this.

DOUBLE JACKS: Two jacks in each of the four suits, also called forty jacks.

DOUBLE JUMP BID: A bid 20 points higher than the previous bid, showing 40 or more points meld. Commonly used in the Florida System and the NPA.

DOUBLE KINGS: Two kings in each of the four suits, also called eighty kings.

DOUBLE PINOCHLE: A meld combination of two queens of spades and two jacks of diamonds, also called double knucks.

DOUBLE RUN: Two aces, two tens, two kings, two queens and two jacks in the trump suit.

DOUBLE QUEENS: Two queens in each of the four suits, also called sixty queens.

DOUBLETON: An initial holding of only two cards in a suit.

DRAWING TRUMP: Playing the trump suit to take out the opponent's trumps.

DROP: To capture an opponent's high card by playing a higher card.

DROP THE BID: To pass or stop bidding abruptly allowing another to have the bid when they are not prepared to take it. E.g. You bid 53 showing 30 meld and you are passed out with the bid when you have no adequate trump suit. (*See also DUMP*)

DUCK: To decline to win a trick which you could have won by playing a higher card.

DUD HAND: Any hand without meld or trick-taking ability.

DUMP: To pass leaving the bid on the dealer.

DUPLICATE BOARD: A card holding device with four pockets to keep the four hands intact for duplicate play.

DUPLICATE PINOCHLE: A form of Pinochle where each hand is duplicated and then played at more than one table.

DUPLICATION OF VALUES: Wasted values in a suit already controlled by partner. E.g. Each partner has a small *Doubleton* in the same suit. Or, one partner has triple aces in a suit that partner is trumping.

EIGHTY KINGS: (*See DOUBLE KINGS*)

ENTRY: A card that provides a means of winning a trick in a particular hand.

ESTABLISH: To set up tricks by driving out winners in the opponent's hands.

ESTABLISHED SUIT: A suit that has been set up so that it now has all winners.

FALSE CARD: A card played to deceive the opponents. [*More likely it is partner who is fooled most often*]

FINESSE: An attempt to win a trick with a card which is lower than that held by RHO but is hoped to be higher than ones held by LHO. For example; you hold ♠A~A~10~10~K~K. Your RHO holds the two tens of spades. The lead comes from him or through him. If he does not play a ten, you play a king, which wins. You FINESSED your king.

FIREHOUSE: The rule in Double-deck mandating that the high bidder must meld a marriage (or flush) in the trump suit he names.

FIT: Combined length between partners of at least 11 cards in a suit.

FLAT HAND: A hand with balanced distribution of cards in each suit. For example: 5 - 5 - 5 - 5, or 6 - 5 - 5 - 4

FLORIDA SYSTEM: A system of bidding and melding commonly used in the NPA, which allows 15 points for a single pinochle and 25 points for a trump sequence or run.

FLUSH: (See RUN)

FOLLOW SUIT: To play a card in the suit that is led.

FORCE: 1. To lead a card which forces an opponent to play a higher card than they might wish.

2. To shorten Declarer's trump holding by making him ruff.

FORCING BID: A bid demanding partner to bid (I.E.: *partner is not expected to pass*)   E.g. Partner opens with 59. This is a forcing bid showing double aces and you should make at least one bid if you have a marriage in your hand.

FORTY JACKS: (*See DOUBLE JACKS*)

GAME: Usually 500 points. (*Unless agreed to differently in advance*).

GAME BID: A bid, which if made, places the team at or above 500.

GET DOWN: To be in position for ones meld to be credited. E.g.: "*Can we get down Partner?*" ["*Do we have at least 20 Meld?*"]   (*See ON BOARD*)

HAND: 1. The cards held by any one player.

      2. A deal of Pinochle.

HAND VALUATION: A method of determining the strength of a hand during the auction. Usually a combination of meld, high card strength and length or shortness of suits.

HCP: High Card Points. (*See COUNTERS*)

HEAD RUB: To turn all twenty tricks in any given hand. A rare event. Named such for the custom of declaring team in that case, to rise from the table and rub the heads of each defender. (*See also BOSTON, BURNED, and TRICKLESS*)

HEADING UP: (*See COVER*)

HIGH CARD POINTS: Any one of the three higher ranking cards played on a trick, ace, ten or king. After each hand all tricks are examined to determine the high card count (HCP.) A team must secure at least 20 HCP to score them, or get credit for any meld. (*See also COUNTERS*)

HOLED: A minus score for a partnership. If the total in meld and high cards won in tricks does not equal or exceed the amount bid, the bidder goes minus or in the hole for that amount. Their meld for that hand and the amount of the bid are subtracted from their running total. They may find themselves in the hole for the amount if they had no previous score; or they may be Holed for the difference between their losing bid and their previous score if the former exceeds the latter. If the score is not sufficient to cover the deficiency, a minus sign is entered to indicate the amount for which the partnership is in the hole.

HONOR CARDS: The ace, ten and king in any suit. (*See also HIGH CARD POINTS and COUNTERS*)

INSUFFICIENT BID: A bid that is not higher than the last valid bid and therefore illegal.

INVITATIONAL BID: Any bid inviting partner to bid again.

JACKS (AROUND): A unit of Meld in which a player shows at least one jack in each suit. This credits 4 to the partnership score. Double Jacks credits 40 and Triple Jacks scores 80.

JUMP BID: Any bid which skips at least one level over the lowest bid possible. When the bidding has gone past the 60 level, a jump of 10 points shows at least 30 points, a jump of 15 shows 40 points, a jump of 20 shows fifty or more points.

JUMP OVERCALL: A bid made at least one level higher than necessary. Usually played as a pre-emptive bid.

KIBITZER: A spectator.

KINGS (AROUND): A unit of Meld in which a player shows at least one king in each suit. This credits 8 to the partnership score. Double Kings Meld credits 80 and. Triple kings scores 160.

KITTY: In Two-handed and Three-handed Pinochle, a set of cards reserved for the high bidders use. The bidder incorporates these cards into his hand and discards an equal amount of cards before play. These discarded cards then become the bidders first trick.

KNUCKS: (*See PINOCHLE*)

LAWS OF DISTRIBUTION: Mathematical tables used to determine the probability of various distributional patterns expressed in percentages.

LEAD: To play the first card on any trick.

LEAD - BACK: A play of a card which signals partner and suggests a suit you want led back to you,

LHO: Left Hand Opponent.

LENGTH POINTS: A method for the bidder to evaluate long suits in a hand which will name trumps. One only values long suits in relation to the suit which is named trump. Therefore if you have few or no trumps, your length counts for nothing.

LIMIT BID: A bid which describes ones high cards and meld within a certain range.

LOCKED SUIT: A suit in which a player has the ability to win the tops no matter who leads the suit. The 'Lock' may be from the beginning or at some point after certain cards have been played. E.g.: "Once he played his ace, I had spades locked."

LONG SUIT: The suit containing the most cards in a given hand.

LOSER: A card or trick, which might be lost to the opponents.

MAKE (A BID OR CONTRACT): To succeed in making enough meld and high cards to fulfill a contract or bid.

MARRIAGE: A unit of Meld in which a player shows the king and queen of any suit. Each marriage credits 2 to the partnership score. A Royal Marriage (king and queen of the trump suit) is credited with 4 points. The Declarer must have a Royal Marriage (or run) in the suit he wishes to make trump. Declarer must put this marriage on the table first when showing the Meld. In any case, the first marriage laid down is perforce the trump suit.

MELD: Any of several combinations of cards laid down at the end of the auction and before the beginning of play. These combinations result in a temporary credit to the partnership. The credit becomes final if the team makes at least 20 HCP during the hand play. If not, the meld is forfeited, and in the case of the bidding team, a penalty is deducted from their score in the amount of the bid.

MELD BID: Any call made during the auction which describes to partner the meld held in ones hand.

MELD OUT: Any meld which places the partnership over the amount needed for game. By prior agreement, this meld may, or may not, end the game. Most rules require that game must be bid rather than melded out. (*See also BID OUT*)

MIS-DEAL: Occurs when at the end of the deal, any player has not received the correct number of cards. If players have not looked at all their cards, the discrepancy may be remedied by passing one or more of the unseen cards to the player who is short. If players have looked at all their cards or if one or more of a players cards have been faced up by the dealer, then the dealer must re-deal. There is no penalty for a mis-deal. Players are responsible for counting their cards before play. If a mis-deal is not discovered before the beginning of play, then the cards stand as dealt.

NEW SUIT: A suit, which has not been previously played in a hand.

NON-COUNTERS: Cards that do not score points when taken on tricks. E.g. Queens and Jacks.

NON-NON: A hand in which the defense is unable to meld and unable to save at least 20 HCP.

NORMAL EXPECTANCY: The average hand one expects to hold in normal circumstances. It may be approximated as 1/3 of the remaining high cards or distribution of a suit when the cards you hold are subtracted.

NORTH: A position in a Pinochle foursome or in a Pinochle diagram opposite South and to the left of West. In duplicate games North keeps the scoring sheet.

NPA: National Pinochle Association.

OFFENSE: The partnership that has made the highest bid and named the trump.

OFF-SUIT: *(See SIDE-SUIT)*

OFFSIDE: A card that is in an unfavorable position; a finesse against it will fail.

ON BOARD: 1. For Declarer, to have sufficient meld which allows Declarer to be in range of making his bid when coupled with HCP. E.g. a bid of 70 with meld of 25 would be ON BOARD, because it is possible to make 45 in HCP.

    2. For defenders, to have a minimum of 20 meld places them ON BOARD, since they only need to make 20 HCP to secure their meld. *(See also GET DOWN)*

ONSIDE: Any card that is in a favorable position to be captured; a finesse against it will succeed.

OPEN THE BIDDING: To make the first bid in an auction.

OPENER: The player making the first bid in an auction.

OPENER'S REBID: The opening bidder's second bid.

OPENING BID: The first bid made during an auction.

OPENING BIDDER: (*See OPENER*)

OPENING LEAD: The card led to the first trick. Declarer makes the opening lead.

OVERCALL: To make a call after opponents have opened the bidding.

OVERRUFF: To play a higher trump when a trick is already ruffed.

PARTNER: The player seated opposite one at the table.

PARTNERSHIP: Two players seated opposite each other at the table.

PASS: A call specifying that a player is permanently out of the auction during that hand.

PASSED HAND: *A player, who had a chance, but chose not to enter the bidding.*

PENALTY: 1. The deduction in score made to a partnership, which has failed to fulfill a contract.

    2. The award of 50 HCP made to a partnership which has verified a RENEGE (or REVOKE) by the opposing team.

PINOCHLE: 1. A unit of Meld in which a player shows the *Jack of Diamonds* and the *Queen of Spades*. This credits 4 to the partnership score. Double Pinochle credits 30 to the partnership score. Triple pinochle scores either 45 or 90. Quadruple pinochle, if saved with 20 HCP, constitutes a game win. The latter two are by prior agreement.

    2. To Run a Pinochle is to complete the game in one hand, either by winning all the tricks, or by saving 20 HCP after melding quadruple pinochle. Pinochle is also referred to as '*KNUCKS*'.

PLAY: 1. The part of the game following the bidding and Meld show, during which the Declarer attempts to make the contract.

    2. To produce a card when it becomes your turn.

POINTS: Awards made on the score sheet to the offense for bidding and fulfilling contracts, and to the defense for showing and saving melds.

POINT COUNT: A method of evaluating a hand which takes into account Meld, high card strength and distribution.

POST-MORTEM: A discussion of a previous hand, wherein a player suggests an alternate bid and/or plays.

PRE-EMPTIVE BID: A high-level jump bid made to deny the opponents room to bid at the lower levels.

PROMOTION: The increase in trick-taking potential of a card in a suit as the higher-ranking cards are played.

PULL: To win an amount of HCP. E.g. *"We pulled 29 on their bid."*

PUMP: To shorten Declarer's trump holding by forcing him to ruff.

QUEENS (AROUND): A unit of Meld in which a player shows at least one queen in each suit, crediting 6 points to the partnership score. Double Queens credits 60 and Triple Queens 120.

RAGGED SUIT: A suit with no trick taking power and no consecutively ranked cards capable of forcing out winners.

RAISE: Accepting partners meld bid by raising the level of bidding.

RANK: Order of precedence in value of cards in a suit. Ace is the highest, then the ten, king, queen and jack which is lowest.

REBID: A second bid by Opener or Responder.

RE-EVALUATION: Upgrading or downgrading the value of your hand based on the previous bidding.

RENEGE: Pronounced [ren-ayg] *(See REVOKE)*

RESPONDER: The partner of an opening bidder, a player sending meld, or of one who has overcalled an opponent.

RETURN: Leading back a suit led at a previous trick.

REVIEW: A restatement of all previous calls, in sequence, given on request.

REVOKE: A failure to follow suit when able to do so. A failure to play a trump when void in a suit led, if able to do so. The failure to HEAD UP (go higher) on any trick when it is your turn. The failure to over-trump on any trick when you are able to do so. Penalty for revoke is loss of all 50 HCP on that hand, plus deduction of the amount of the bid from partnership score if you are the declaring team. (*Also known as RENEGE*)

RHO: Right Hand Opponent.

ROUNDHOUSE: A unit of Meld in which a player shows at least one king and queen in each suit, crediting 24 to team score. Note that a ROUNDHOUSE when combined with a *RUN* in the trump suit only counts as 35 points (*not the expected 39 points from 15 for the RUN plus 24 for the ROUNDHOUSE*) since a single ROYAL MARRIAGE can only be counted once in the run and not again in the ROUNDHOUSE. Double roundhouse Meld credits 240 to the team score.

ROYAL MARRIAGE: A king and queen in the trump suit which counts for 4 Meld points.

ROYALTIES: Melds of Double Queens or higher, which some house rules stipulate must be bid in their entirety after the second bid. E.g. A player holding 80 kings and a run, opens the bidding at 50. An opponent bids 51, Opener bids 52, opponent bids 53, Opener making his third bid, must now bid 80, thus revealing his royalties.

RUFF: To play a trump on a trick when void in the suit led.

RUFFING: Trumping a suit in which you are void.

RUN: A unit of Meld in which a player shows a complete sequence of cards in the trump suit. Ace, ten, king, queen and jack. This credits 15 to the partnership score. Double RUN credits 150 to the partnership score. See also: BARE RUN.

SACRIFICE BID: A defensive bid usually made with expectation of loss that is hoped to be less than the opponents could make if allowed to take the bid. Sometimes it creates the chance that opponents will bid one level higher than they are able to fulfill.

SAFETY PLAY: A play of the cards in a way that ensures that your contract succeeds.

SANDBAG: To deliberately delay the play of winning cards when you first have the chance. A characteristic of most winning players, disparaged by most novices.

SAVE: 1. To make the bid as Declarer.

2. To pull at least 20 points as the non-bidding team.

3. To bid the minimum when partner is the dealer and may have meld with no biddable suit.

SCORE SHEET: The paper on which points won or lost are recorded. This sheet is usually divided with a vertical line down the middle labeled US and THEM, and shows the amount of each bid as well as the dealer.

SCRATCH: To make at least 31 HCP as bidder and thus prevent the non-bidding team from saving.

SECOND HAND: 1. In bidding, the dealer's partner.

2. In play, the second player to play to a trick.

SECOND TRUMP: Declarer's secondary suit capable of turning all tricks once the trump suit is exhausted.

SEQUENCE: (*See RUN*)

SET (THE BID, THE CONTRACT): To defeat the bid or contract. (*See also BETE*)

SHAPE: The distribution or number of cards held in each suit.

SHUFFLE: To mix the cards in the deck preparatory to dealing.

SHOW OUT: Fail to follow suit. (*See also REVOKE, RENEGE*)

SIDE SUIT: A suit other than the suit named by Declarer as trumps.

SIGNAL: To give information about your hand through the cards which you play.

SINGLETON: An initial holding of one card in a suit.

SIXTY QUEENS: (*See DOUBLE QUEENS*)

SLEEPER: The belated play of an ace by a player presumed not to have had the card.

SLUFF: The discard of a worthless card.

SMEAR: To play a counter or honor on a trick in anticipation that it could potentially be won by partner.

SOLID SUIT: A suit with at least six of the top eight cards in sequence. (E.g. *A~A~A~A~10~10~Q~Q in the same suit.*)

SOUTH: A position in a Pinochle diagram opposite North and to the left of East. In Pinochle diagrams South is usually depicted as the Declarer for ease of reading, continuity and convenience.

SPLIT DECK: When each team earns exactly 25 HCP.

SQUEEZE: To lead a card that compels an opponent to discard a winner or unguard a suit.

STIFF: Holding only the card or cards mentioned in a suit. E.g.: *"I had the ace of clubs stiff."* Or, *"My partner had a stiff marriage in diamonds."*

STOPPER: A card which prevents the opponents from winning a series of tricks in a particular suit.

STRENGTH: The trick taking ability of a hand.

SUITS: The four divisions of cards in a deck along with the symbols, which designate them. These are Spades (♠), Hearts (♥), Clubs (♣) and Diamonds (♦). In double-deck Pinochle each suit is equal in rank except for the one named as trump on a particular hand.

SUPPORT: The number of cards held in a suit that partner makes trump. (*See also FIT*)

SURE TRICK: A trick that can be taken without giving up the lead to an opponent.

TEMPO: Timing which establishes your objective before the opponents can counter it to gain theirs.

TENACE: [*pronounced ten-ace*] A holding of honor cards not quite in sequence. E.g.: You hold ♠A~A~10~10~K~K. You are missing two tens. If your RHO holds the tens, and the suit is led toward you, your kings will win if he does not play his tens; thus you hold a TENACE over the RHO. In short, his tens can be FINESSED. (*See also FINESSE*)

THREE-SUITER: A hand with at least six cards in each of three suits, distributed 6 - 6 - 6 - 2, 7 - 6 - 6 - 1, or 7 - 7 - 6 - 0.

THIRD HAND: 1. In bidding, the last player to bid before the dealer's first bid.

2. In play, the leader's partner.

THROUGH, TO LEAD: Leading through a holding of high cards held by your LHO.

THROW-OFF: A discard made when void in a suit and having no trumps. E.g.: *"I had a chance to throw-off my losing diamonds on your trumps."* (*See also* DISCARD)

TOPS: Winners or top cards in a suit.

TOWARD, TO LEAD: Leading towards your partner's high cards.

TRAPPING: A technique for building tricks by making an opponent play his card before you select your card. E.g.: *"I had him trapped, if he pitched the club, I would throw-off the spade. If he got rid of the spade, I would ditch my club."*

TRICK: A combination of four cards, one contributed by each player in clockwise rotation, beginning with the lead. E.g.: *"I knew you won the trick, but I had no counter to give you."*

TRICK SCORE: The points scored for high cards played on tricks. Does not include meld.

TRICKLESS: To win all 20 tricks in any given hand is to pull a trickless. By prior agreement, this feat since rare, can be agreed to end the game no matter what the previous scores were. E.g. *"We almost had a trickless but my partner blew it with a wrong throw-off."* (*See also* HEAD RUB, BURNED)

TRIPLETON: An initial holding of only three cards in a suit.

TRUMP: To play a ranking suit card when void in the suit led.

TRUMP SUIT: That suit named by Declarer which outranks all other suits for that particular hand. E.g.: *"I wanted to get in the bidding but my trump suit was too shoddy."*

TRUMPING: Playing a trump card when one is void in the suit led. E.g.: *"You must have forgot he was trumping hearts."*

TWO SUITER: A hand with at least seven cards in one suit and 6 cards or more in another suit.

UNBLOCK: To purposely throw-off a winning card or high card to avoid blocking a suit in which partner has winners. To throw off a card which would force partner. E.g. You hold 10~K~J in trumps. Declarer leads A~A. On the second ace you play the ten, not the king. If partner has A~10~K~Q~Q your unblocking the ten avoids forcing his ace on the third round of trumps since you have already played your ten.

UNDERBIDDER: A player known to chronically bid less than the value of his hand, usually because of a reluctance to be set.

UNDERLEAD: To lead away from a hand in which you hold the top card. E.g. *"The only way I could get my ace in, was for you to underlead yours."*

UNGUARDED: 1. An unprotected high card that if not played first, can be caught by an equally ranked card.

2. A suit in which you have no guard or stoppers.

UP TO, TO LEAD: Leading toward the second consecutive player's high cards.

UPPERCUT: To ruff with a high trump forcing a player to overruff with a higher trump thus promoting a trump winner for partner.

Review the following example. Spades are trumps, you are West holding the cards showing in the following figure (also showing South's hand and your partner, East's cards);

When you lead a heart, your partner must trump with the king; this promotes your ten to a winner since South must OVERRUFF with Ace or Ten. If East timidly trumps with the queen, your side turns no more tricks.

VALUATION: A method of determining the value of a particular hand during the auction. Usually a combination of Shape (distribution) High cards and melds.

VOID: An initial holding of no cards in a particular suit. E.g. *"I knew one of you were coming in spades because I was void."*

WALK: To take a trick with a card not normally expected to win. Often the last trick.

WASTED VALUES: Values which are duplicated in the partnership hands. This could occur if one partner is void of a suit in which the other has aces, or, if both are trumping the same suit.

WEIGHT, TAKE THE: An initial minimum opening bid of 50. E.g. A player might say: *"I'll take the weight."* Instead of: *"I bid 50."*

WIPE-OFF: The provision in Double-deck which allows a team's Meld to be erased when they fail to score at least 20 in HCPs.

YAHOOED: When playing on the Internet, to be ejected involuntarily from the game server while a game is in progress. Also, to be the recipient of a long string of computer generated hands containing very little meld or playing potential. Meanwhile, maybe the opponents are receiving hands with large royalties.

YARBOROUGH: A hand with no trick taking value and no meld.

244

INDEX

Q.

R.

S.

T.

U.

V.

W.

X.

Y.

MELD TABLE

Meld Combinations		1x	2x	3x	4x
PINOCHLE	(Q♠ and J◊)	4[2]	30	45/90[5]	
JACKS	(around)	4	40	80	160
QUEENS	(around)	6	60	120	240
KINGS	(around)	8	80	160	320
ACES	(around)	10	100	200	400
RUN	(sequence in trump suit)	15[2]	150	300	600
ROUNDHOUSE[3]		24	240	*CT*	
RUN + ROUNDHOUSE		35[4]	*CT*		
MARRIAGE	(K/Q pair)	2	4	6	8
ROYAL MARRIAGE	(K/Q trump)	4	8	12	16

Notes:

1. Meld values vary based on organization guidelines (such as within the NPA), implemented rules (such as the Yahoo! Game site), or local custom (a friends kitchen table). Check for local variances when playing in unfamiliar localities.

2. In the Florida System as played in the NPA, a single Run scores 25 points and a single Pinochle scores as 15 points. Counts for other combinations may vary accordingly.

3. Roundhouse is the accepted term for a combination of King and Queen in each suit.

4. The combination of a trump Run and Roundhouse is usually accepted as 35 points, not the anticipated 39 points. Here the trump marriage (king and queen) is only counted once, so 4 points is subtracted from the count.

5. As agreed upon in advance of play or local acceptance.

6. Meld combinations listed as *CT* are only possible in three handed Pinochle (Cut Throat) so values are not shown.

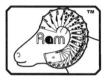

Pinochle Press - *Order Form*
Pinochle Literature and Supplies

Order by Mail:

Pinochle Press
P.O. Box 120040
St. Albans, NY 11412

Order by phone
or by fax:

888-LRoyRam
  (888-576-9726)

Order online: www.pinochlepress.com
Order by email: sales@pinochlepress.com

To order: *Complete reverse side and address information indicated below and submit as indicated above.*

Check our website regularly for more products and up to date prices, as well as tips, cartoons and news articles for those who want to really play Pinochle, and other card games.

Please: *Provide all of the information requested below to expedite the processing of your order:*

Ship to Name: _____
Address: _____
_____
City, State, Zip: _____
Phone: _____
Email: _____

Comments: _____
_____
_____
_____
_____

Privacy Statement: We will not sell or provide personal information to any other organization, but request it in case there are any issues or questions regarding your order. You are welcome to leave the phone and email information blank, however if there are any problems with your order it may take us longer to process if we cannot contact you. Thank you for your order.   **Form: PPB0408**

Pinochle Press - *ORDER BLANK*
Pinochle Literature and Supplies

Item Description	Qty	Each	Total
The Complete Guide to Double Deck Pinochle by L. Roy Ram - Hardcover 256 pages		$24.95	
The Complete Guide to Double Deck Pinochle by L. Roy Ram - Softcover 256 pages		$16.95	
The Complete Guide to Double Deck Pinochle by L. Roy Ram-Softcover 256 pages largeprint		$19.95	
Pinochle Tips and Strategies by Anthony Collins		$14.95	
Pinochle is the Name of the Game by Walter Gibson		$5.95	
Ram's Deluxe Plastic Coated Pinochle Cards Double Deck 80 cards - Circle **Red** or **Blue** backs		$5.95	
Ram's Deluxe Plastic Coated Pinochle Cards 2 Double Decks 80 cards - 1 each Red & Blue backs		$9.95	
Solid Hardwood Card box- Circle **Light**, **Dark** or **Red** (*holds two Double-Decks,score pad and pencil - **not included**)*		$39.95	
Boxed set - Circle **Light**, **Dark** or **Red** (*includes-* Hardwood box, 2 Double-Decks - Red & Blue, scorepad, pencil and softcover **Complete Guide to Double-Deck Pinochle**)		$59.95	
Sub-total from above items			
Shipping & Handling $5.00 (***orders over $50 no charge***)			
New York State Residents add Sales Tax at 8.25%			
Total Amount for Entire Order			

Payment Method: ☐ **Check / Money Order** ☐ **American Express**
☐ **Visa** ☐ **Mastercard** ☐ **Discover**

Credit Card: [_ _ _ _] [_ _ _ _] [_ _ _ _] [_ _ _ _] Expires: ___/___

Signature: _____

Notice: If a credit card is used for payment, the signature above is required for the order to be processed. All personal check orders will be shipped complete after the check has cleared. Orders will normally be processed in 7-14 days, but will not be shipped incomplete without special instructions. All prices are subject to change without notice, and availability of items may cause delays in processing. Check online for the latest products, up to date prices and availability of items listed above, as well as volume discounts.

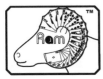

Pinochle Press - *Order Form*
Pinochle Literature and Supplies

Order by Mail:
Pinochle Press
P.O. Box 120040
St. Albans, NY 11412

Order by phone
    or by fax: 888-LRoyRam
                 (888-576-9726)
Order online: www.pinochlepress.com
Order by email: sales@pinochlepress.com

To order: *Complete reverse side and address information indicated below and submit as indicated above.*

Check our website regularly for more products and up to date prices, as well as tips, cartoons and news articles for those who want to really play Pinochle, and other card games.

Please: *Provide all of the information requested below to expedite the processing of your order:*

Ship to Name: _____
Address: _____
_____
City, State, Zip: _____
Phone: _____
Email: _____

Comments: _____
_____
_____
_____
_____

Privacy Statement: We will not sell or provide personal information to any other organization, but request it in case there are any issues or questions regarding your order. You are welcome to leave the phone and email information blank, however if there are any problems with your order it may take us longer to process if we cannot contact you. Thank you for your order.   **Form: PPB0408**

Pinochle Press - *ORDER BLANK*
Pinochle Literature and Supplies

Item Description	Qty	Each	Total
The Complete Guide to Double Deck Pinochle by L. Roy Ram - Hardcover 256 pages		$24.95	
The Complete Guide to Double Deck Pinochle by L. Roy Ram - Softcover 256 pages		$16.95	
The Complete Guide to Double Deck Pinochle by L. Roy Ram-Softcover 256 pages largeprint		$19.95	
Pinochle Tips and Strategies by Anthony Collins		$14.95	
Pinochle is the Name of the Game by Walter Gibson		$5.95	
Ram's Deluxe Plastic Coated Pinochle Cards Double Deck 80 cards - Circle **Red** or **Blue** backs		$5.95	
Ram's Deluxe Plastic Coated Pinochle Cards 2 Double Decks 80 cards - 1 each Red & Blue backs		$9.95	
Solid Hardwood Card box- Circle **Light, Dark** or **Red** (*holds two Double-Decks, score pad and pencil - **not included**)		$39.95	
Boxed set - Circle **Light, Dark** or **Red** (*includes-* Hardwood box, 2 Double-Decks - Red & Blue, scorepad, pencil and softcover **Complete Guide to Double-Deck Pinochle**)		$59.95	
Sub-total from above items			
Shipping & Handling $5.00 (**orders over $50 no charge**)			
New York State Residents add Sales Tax at 8.25%			
Total Amount for Entire Order			

Payment Method: ☐ **Check / Money Order** ☐ **American Express**
☐ **Visa** ☐ **Mastercard** ☐ **Discover**

Credit Card: [_ _ _ _] [_ _ _ _] [_ _ _ _] [_ _ _ _] Expires: ___/___

Signature: _____

Notice: If a credit card is used for payment, the signature above is required for the order to be processed. All personal check orders will be shipped complete after the check has cleared. Orders will normally be processed in 7-14 days, but will not be shipped incomplete without special instructions. All prices are subject to change without notice, and availability of items may cause delays in processing. Check online for the latest products, up to date prices and availability of items listed above, as well as volume discounts.